GENEALOGIST'S REFERENCE SHELF

Publish Your Family History

Preserving Your Heritage in a Book

SUSAN YATES AND GREG IOANNOU

DUNDURN PRESS
TORONTO

Editors: Heather Ball, Andrea Battiston, Jennie Worden
Printer: Webcom

Library and Archives Canada Cataloguing in Publication

Yates, Susan
  Publish your family history : preserving your heritage in a book / by Susan Yates and Greg Ioannou.

(Genealogist's Reference Shelf)
Co-published by the Ontario Genealogical Society.

Includes index.
ISBN 978-1-55488-727-9

    1. Genealogical literature--Publishing. 2. Self-publishing. 3. Book design. I. Ioannou, Greg, 1953- II. Ontario Genealogical Society III. Title.

Z285.5.Y38 2010   070.5'93   C2009-907465-6

1   2   3   4   5   14   13   12   11   10

 Conseil des Arts du Canada   **Canada Council for the Arts**   Canada  **ONTARIO ARTS COUNCIL CONSEIL DES ARTS DE L'ONTARIO**

We acknowledge the support of the **Canada Council for the Arts** and the **Ontario Arts Council** for our publishing program. We also acknowledge the financial support of the **Government of Canada** through the **Canada Book Fund** and **The Association for the Export of Canadian Books**, and the **Government of Ontario** through the **Ontario Book Publishers Tax Credit program**, and the **Ontario Media Development Corporation**.

Care has been taken to trace the ownership of copyright material used in this book. The author and the publisher welcome any information enabling them to rectify any references or credits in subsequent editions.

J. Kirk Howard, President

Printed and bound in Canada.
www.dundurn.com

Ontario Genealogical Society
Suite 102, 40 Orchard View Boulevard
Toronto, Ontario, Canada M4R 1B9
tel. (416) 489-0734   fax. (416) 489-9803
provoffice@ogs.on.ca   www.ogs.on.ca

Dundurn Press	Gazelle Book Services Limited	Dundurn Press
3 Church Street, Suite 500	White Cross Mills	2250 Military Road
Toronto, Ontario, Canada	High Town, Lancaster, England	Tonawanda, NY
M5E 1M2	LA1 4XS	U.S.A. 14150

CONTENTS

ACKNOWLEDGMENTS

Thanks to all the people who helped pull this book together: Ruth Chernia at the Ontario Genealogical Society (who came up with the idea and has fostered the project throughout), and the following people at Colborne Communications: Heather Ball, Andrea Battiston, Rachel Rosen and Jennie Worden.

Susan Yates
Greg Ioannou

CHAPTER 1

SHARING
YOUR
RESEARCH

Researching family history is, for most of us, a labour of love. You are exploring your own background and the backgrounds of the people who mean the most to you. Many people reach a point where they want to share what they have found with their loved ones. The traditional way to do so is to put it all into the form of a book.

The whole notion of preparing a book is daunting. For one thing, books are long. Just writing a book is usually a huge undertaking. (We can tell you that with confidence. This is, after all, only the second paragraph of this book—we know we have a l-o-n-g way to go!) With a family history, even when you've finished writing, you are faced with what can seem like an insurmountable group of tasks that you likely know little about: editing, design, typesetting, printing, binding, distribution.

Most people who want to publish a book follow a pretty traditional route: They write the manuscript and send it to agents or publishers, who send it straight back. It is an easy, if depressing, way to accumulate a fine collection of rejection letters. Perhaps luckily, that route isn't open to the writers of family histories. Few traditional publishers will consider publishing them, unless perhaps you are related to the Kennedys or Churchills.

There is another way, however, one that is open to more and more people, particularly because new technologies are making it cheaper and easier: publishing it yourself. This book explores the various ways of doing just that. We can help you publish your book, whether it is intended for a handful of close relatives or for a wider audience.

This book is designed for people who want to do it themselves, especially those whose publishing projects are on a small scale. Rather than using the term "self-publishing," which has connotations of "no one wanted to publish the thing so I just did it myself," we've used "home publishing," to reflect the fact that most publishing projects outside of the mainstream book publishing industry are small-scale labours of love.

Your book can be handmade or professionally bound, can be handwritten or elaborately typeset. You can tailor the look—and the cost—to your particular needs and the needs of your readers. This book will lead you through the various options.

WHY DO YOU WANT TO PUBLISH A BOOK?

First things first. Even though you aren't going to be taking your family history to a traditional publisher, there is still a lot you can learn from how publishers operate. Let's ask some of the questions that publishers would ask of your manuscript. They are questions that need to be asked of any publishing project.

What Are You Trying to Communicate?

Many publishing projects don't really work because they have no central idea. Until that central idea has been thought through clearly, there is no point even starting to write the book. Many publishing projects should be shot down before they start, because the writer has no particular reason (other than ego gratification) for writing the book.

That applies to family histories too. Family histories range all the way from very dry family trees with little or no text to raunchy "all the family dirt you were scared to ask about" exposés. (One of the authors of this book has an aunt who, in her eighties, wrote a family history in which she was very explicit about exactly what she thought of various members of the family, and "set the record straight" about various events in the family's history. It makes wonderful reading—for some family members, anyway.)

A book with a weak central idea can often be improved by recasting that idea. For example, imagine that you have spent a lot of time researching your family tree and gathering documents related to your family's history. You decide to gather all of your research together to preserve it for the rest of the family. Your plan is to print out the family tree, then copies of all the documents sorted by type of document, and put it all into three-ring binders and give the binders to the members of your family.

Your family members' eyes have always glazed over when you've shown them parts of the family tree, and have shown little interest in helping with your research. How likely are they to ever make any use of the binders?

The only way you have ever been able to get the family interested in your research is by telling them anecdotes about obscure relatives, like the time cousin Eustace woke up convinced he'd inherited the Taj Mahal, and immediately left for India to claim his inheritance. That pretty much tells you what you have to do to prepare a family history that will preserve your research and that the family will treasure: combine the research with whatever you've been able to find out about the life stories of the people in your family.

Who Are You Trying to Reach?

There are various potential audiences for your book. The most obvious audience is your family. That doesn't mean just your immediate family: in theory, virtually every (living) person mentioned in your book will have some interest in it. Some other audiences:

- genealogical societies in the areas where branches of your family live
- local history societies in those same areas
- public libraries in places where there are lots of members of your family
- genealogists working on families that somewhat overlap with yours

What Interests Those Audiences?

Many family histories are really just reprinted research notes or family trees. The best ones go far beyond that. The writers have tried to bring the family's history to life in a way that will really reach the readers.

The best way to do this is to try as much as possible to tell the various stories you have uncovered about the people in the family. Where did people live? Why did they move there? What was the place like? What did they do for a living? What were their lives like? How did they live, relax, work, worship, die? How did they fit into their community?

Think how novelists bring their characters and their stories to life. Look at the detail a good novelist will provide on the people, the settings they lived in, the things they did. You have an advantage over a novelist: you are describing real people, and you have documentary evidence of what they were like.

Feel free to include the most interesting bits of that evidence: maps, photos of people and places, newspaper clippings, letters—anything that helps bring the people to life. Try to vary the things you reproduce. Photos of people are great, but it gets a bit boring if all you show are formal wedding photos.

Think of how to organize the book so that it flows for a reader. Some family histories organize their material by town. Some, by who the people are descended from. Some, by looking at key people in the family's story.

Put yourself in the position of each person in the book who is likely to read it. How is your cousin Lucretia going to feel when you spend three pages telling her brother Nigel's story, then say, "Nigel also had a sister called Lucretia"? Many writers, sad to say, focus closely on the husbands they describe and then dismiss the wives with a quick mention.

Remember also that people in the future will be using your book as a resource as they research other family histories. You should try to tell your family's stories—but you are also reporting your research findings, and they should be as accurate and complete as you can make them.

Is a Book the Right Vehicle?

Books have enormous strengths and terrible weaknesses. You should ask yourself whether some other medium might be more appropriate. Do you have enough material for a book? Is a book the right format to get that material into your readers' hands?

Books' Strengths	Books' Weaknesses
• durable—can last for centuries	• difficult to update and revise
• inexpensive if printed in sufficient quantities	• can be expensive in small quantities
• portable	• heavy and bulky in quantity
• impressive if designed and edited well	• mortifying if poorly done
• long—enough space to thoroughly explore an idea or topic	• long—can seem endless if the idea or topic was more suited to a magazine article

For a family history, the first item in these lists usually trumps everything else: books are durable. They can be handed from generation to generation as treasured heirlooms in a way that no other available medium can.

Is the Internet an Alternative?

So, what about the Internet as a technological solution? Well, the point about publishing in cyberspace is that it doesn't give you a book of your own. A virtual book lacks the physical presence that real paper, ink and binding delivers.

However, the Internet can provide a perfect solution for some. You can make your family history available to your family, wherever they may be, at no cost to them. And you can make the history into a living document so that your relatives can update the information.

There are several ways to publish your material on the Internet. For any of them, you'll need to get some web space, and a web address, from your Internet provider. Almost all Internet accounts come with some space and addresses included. Your options include:

A PDF file: PDF is a file format that allows people to view and print your document the way you intended it to look.

When preparing a PDF, you design the pages as you would design book pages. (See Chapter 5 for ideas on page design.) Once the book has been laid out, you use PDF software to convert the file to a PDF. With the PDF file, you in effect upload the book, in book format, to the Internet and just let people download it and print out their own sets of pages. Be sure when creating the PDF that you embed the required fonts, so that it will look the way you intended when people view and print it. An Internet search on "PDF software" will guide you to the latest software for creating PDFs.

An RTF document: Like a PDF, an RTF (Rich Text Format) document will allow any user to download and read your family history. It doesn't allow for fancy formatting or graphics, but it creates small files, and almost any program on almost any computer system will be able to read it.

A traditional website: There are many software programs that you can use to design and upload your site. Writing for the web is very different than writing a book. In many ways, it is ideal for a family history. You can organize the site like a family tree, and have the user click on each person in the tree for more details—perhaps a bio and some images. You can incorporate search features into the site to help the user find a specific family member or find relatives from a certain place or era.

When you're creating a website, pay close attention to how you structure your information. It does no good to have pages and pages of text (or worse—one page crammed with too much information and no paragraph breaks!) if you don't give your reader a quick and easy way to find what he or she is looking for. Break your information into short chunks and organize it into logical categories. For example, if one branch of your family immigrated to Canada and another stayed in Tanzania, it might make sense to use geography to organize the site. If your research dates back to the 15th century, you could structure your information in chronological order.

A good principle is that a user should never have to visit more than three pages after the home page of a site to get the information that he or she wants. After more than that, the reader tends to lose interest or get frustrated.

A wiki: A "wiki" is a type of online document that is collectively created and maintained. Anyone can edit it, even someone with no knowledge of HTML. The design is kept as simple and easy-to-use as possible. The wiki format can also work well, particularly if your relatives want to participate in keeping the information up-to-date. This means that if Aunt Edna unexpectedly discovers a shoebox in the attic full of the letters great-uncle James wrote during World War II, she can add that content to the family history without sending it to you first.

Who Will Want the Book?

Because you are publishing the book yourself, you aren't constrained by the need to sell a huge number of copies, but you do need to think through how many copies you are likely to distribute, who you want to have the book and how to reach that readership. Chapter 11 looks at these questions.

Can You Write?

You're probably the wrong person to ask. Many wonderful writers are too aware of their shortcomings, and many awful writers are unaware that they have any shortcomings.

But the writing quality of the original manuscript is a factor in any publishing project. You probably should budget for some editing help, even if you're a good writer.

How Risky is It?

The classic failed home-publishing venture costs far more than the publisher expected. Often the net result is a thinner bank account and a basement full of books. We'll try to lead you to ways to save money and keep a lid on costs. Many home-publishing ventures bring in only a small fraction of the publisher's most pessimistic income projection. Uncle Ignatz may never come through with the $5,000 contribution to the costs that he keeps promising. To be safe, when you calculate your projected revenues, assume the worst—and be honest with yourself. Then, when you are doing a final budget, use half of that worst-case income projection. If the project is still affordable, go ahead!

So Why Would Anyone of Sound Mind Consider Home Publishing?

The traditional publishers will pay you for your manuscript and promote it professionally. Do it yourself and you get all of the costs and potentially huge hassles. Why bother? For all sorts of good reasons.

Control. Talk to many writers, and they'll tell you: "People thought my book was a Harlequin with that cover they put on it"; "Why did they change the name of my family history to Attack of the Aardvark Lizards?"; and "The page design is so confusing I can't even find the page numbers."

Low overhead and lower break-even point. Many perfectly wonderful home-publishing projects just aren't financially viable for book publishing firms. A family history that will sell only 200 copies will not appeal to even the smallest small press (unless it came with a grant of some sort to publish it), but can make a worthwhile home-publishing venture, because the home publisher doesn't have to carry all of the overhead of trying to produce and distribute a full list of books. Printing 200 copies of that family history book and distributing them to the members of the clan can make considerable financial sense.

Flexibility. Want to produce a book that can be printed in tiny quantities on archival-quality paper with lots of photos? Traditional publishing doesn't want to know you exist.

Creativity. Want your book to have a hand-embossed cover, handmade paper pages, and a creatively stitched binding? You may well have the time available to invest in producing such a labour of love. Sometimes you are the only person who can give a project the love and care it deserves.

Publish it yourself and it will come out the way you wanted it to (give or take your own abilities and budget, and if the printers are willing!).

CHAPTER 2

PUBLISHING
BASICS

Knowing how traditional publishing works will help guide your home-publishing project. Because most home-publishing projects involve most of the steps used in traditional publishing, this chapter will give a quick overview of the traditional publishing process.

PRINTERS, PUBLISHERS, VANITY PRESSES, CONTRACT PUBLISHERS AND PACKAGERS

Many people confuse publishers and printers, and get even more confused when you mention vanity presses, contract publishers and packagers. Here is how to tell them apart:

- A *printer* prints books. If you take your publishing project to a printer, the printer will (for a fee) print up the number of copies you specify and deliver them to you.
- A *publisher*, as you might guess, publishes books. Publishers buy the rights to the book from the author (usually paying a royalty, which is an amount paid to the author for every copy sold); arrange to

have the book edited, designed and printed; advertise the book; and distribute it (which means getting it into bookstores, book clubs and so on).

- A *vanity press* is sort of like a publisher, with one major difference: the author pays the publisher, rather than the publisher paying the author. If a publisher offers to publish your book for a fee, be careful. Vanity presses have a well-earned poor reputation, which they built by overcharging authors, printing shoddy books, printing very few copies, spending nothing on advertising or promotion and having little or no ability to distribute the book.

- A *contract publisher* will also publish your book for you for a fee. Unlike vanity presses, contract publishers will specify the editing, design and printing charges in advance, and will not normally offer to advertise the book or distribute it for you. A contract publisher might be a good choice if you really don't want to do it yourself. You can find them listed in the Yellow Pages under Publishers' Services.

- *Print on demand (POD)* is the new kid on the block, and is perfect for many family history books. How print on demand works is simple: you send the computer files for your book to the POD company, along with a relatively modest cheque. For the fee, the POD company sends you a small number of copies of the book, and advertises your book on their website. Whenever someone orders a copy of the book (at a price you specify) the POD company collects their payment, prints a copy of the book and mails it to the buyer. Every so often the POD company sends you a cheque for your share of the money collected. No muss, little fuss, no cartons of books mouldering in your attic.

- A *packager* prepares books for book publishers. The packager usually pays for the writing, editing, design and printing. The publisher pays the packager a per-book rate for the books, and advertises and distributes them. Packagers usually come up with the book ideas and sell them to publishers, so packagers are unlikely to be interested in your book idea. It may, in certain circumstances, be possible to sell your book to a publisher as a package—which is how this book was produced.

COPYRIGHT

Copyright means exactly what it says: whoever owns the copyright on a publication has the sole right to make copies of it. If you own the copyright on material, no one else can use it in any form, whether print, electronic or otherwise, without your permission.

Likewise, you cannot publish copyrighted material without the permission of the copyright holder. Copyright is usually, but not necessarily, held by the author of the work. If you want to reproduce copyrighted material in your own book, you should contact the publisher of the original work to obtain permission. Remember that copyright is not just for writing: It extends to design, illustration and photographs as well.

In Canada, you automatically hold copyright to anything you have written, and you do not need to renew that copyright. The copyright lasts for 51 years after you die. If you own the copyright to a publishable work, your will should specify who will inherit it should you die.

If your book will reproduce anyone else's work, you should ensure that you have the copyright holder's permission to reproduce it. That doesn't apply to such things as old family photos. It is going to be perfectly fine to reproduce a clipping from an 1865 newspaper in your family history. But a 1965 clipping will still be copyrighted and you'll need permission to reproduce it.

When the copyright expires, the work becomes "public domain," which means that anyone can reprint it without paying any fee to the copyright holder.

EDITORIAL

There is wide variation in how editorial departments in publishing houses are organized. Chapter 4 of this book examines the editorial function more closely. For the purposes of this quick overview, it is enough to note that the editorial department acquires, edits and proofreads the book. In doing so, the editors usually deal with the production and sales department.

Since you're taking care of these functions yourself, your home-publishing project will demand that you ask the following questions about the manuscript:

- Who will offer an impartial evaluation of the book's organization and writing?
- Does it need a structural edit?
- Who will copyedit the book?
- Who will proofread the book?
- Does the book need an index?
- Who will arrange for an ISBN and for the CIP data? (see box on Editorial Legalities)

EDITORIAL LEGALITIES: Getting Your Book's
ISBN and CIP and Registering it with Library and Archives Canada

Library and Archives Canada keeps track of all the books published in the country. It assigns each publisher a list of ten-digit (soon to be 13-digit) International Standard Book Numbers (ISBN). The ISBN of a book is its unique fingerprint, identifying a single publisher and publication, and is embedded in the bar code on the back of the book. No two books in the world are ever registered under the same ISBN (unless someone at the publishing house or filing office has made a terrific mistake!).

If you simply plan to distribute your print run to family and friends, you won't need an ISBN. However, if your hopes stretch farther afield and you want to make your home-published book available to the book trade (be it to bookstores, wholesalers or libraries) you'll absolutely need to obtain an ISBN before you go to press. It's essential to the distribution, sales and tracking process in the industry.

The same application process applies whether you're a huge book publisher or only ever plan to sell a hundred books. The office will need the publisher's name, even if it's the same as yours, and a title. Happily, registering your book is free and can be completed in a matter of hours. You can get an application by calling Library and Archives Canada's Canadian ISBN Agency at (819) 994-6872.

After you've acquired an ISBN, you'll need to get its close cousin assigned to your book: the Cataloguing in Publication (CIP) data. The CIP data gets included on the copyright page on the back of the title page. While the ISBN only reveals a book's publisher, title and language of publication (if you can crack the code), the CIP data is far more descriptive. A book's CIP information is very similar to what you would find in a library catalogue, including subject headings and classification numbers. When you apply for CIP data, the office creates a bibliographic record on a database that is linked to various bibliographic products, used by wholesalers, booksellers and libraries around the world. What this means is that you may get a whole lot of unwanted phone calls if you're intending to market your book only to family members, so be forewarned.

You can request the CIP form at the same time as you get your ISBN application, but remember that you'll need the ISBN first. You can also get the CIP form online at www.collectionscanada/cip/index-e.html. Because the CIP cataloguing process is more involved, allow two weeks for it to be completed. The central CIP office will tell you where to send the CIP form in your area.

PRODUCTION

The production department of a publishing company typically deals with budgets and schedules as well as design, layout and printing. Obviously, these are all major areas of the publishing process, and each will be dealt with in depth later in this book.

Production is one of the main areas that derail home-publishing ventures. Desktop publishing software has made it very easy to prepare book pages very badly. Small local print shops have made it easy to print up bound sets of those badly designed pages very shoddily. One of the main goals of this book is to point out the major book-production pitfalls. Questions to ask yourself about production include:

- Should I use offset or digital or handmade?
- Who will design the cover?
- How many colours will appear on the cover?
- Who will design the pages?
- Will there be any use of colour, illustrations or photographs inside the book?
- Who will lay out the pages?
- Who will print the book?
- How many copies should be printed?
- What paper stock should be used to print it?

GETTING HELP

The book publishing industry is a maze of associations, some of which can be very useful to the home publisher. The Editors' Association of Canada's website has an especially helpful section on publishing associations at **www.editors.ca/web/assoc.htm**. (Inevitably, some of the association web addresses below will go out of date quite quickly. The EAC site will provide you with up-to-date links, and also has links to non-Canadian resources.)

Some home publishers find they really need professional help with book design, editing or some other aspect of the publishing process. It is often worth the expense of bringing on a pro to help with the aspects that are giving you the most trouble. And, of course, if your budget is big enough you can have professionals do a lot of the work for you.

Some associations that offer useful services to Canadian home publishers are:

- Alcuin Society (**www.alcuinsociety.com**) is a Canadian organization for people with a broad range of interests concerning books and publishing, including the book arts of printing, binding, paper-making, calligraphy and illustration.
- The Canadian Association of Photographers and Illustrators in Communications (CAPIC) maintains a database of CAPIC members by style and specialty. It is used to responding to enquiries from potential clients about book and magazine photographers and illustrators. (**www.capic.org**)
- The Canadian Authors Association, which has branches nation-wide, offers meetings, workshops and an annual conference to published and unpublished writers. CAA is an excellent resource if you need help polishing your writing. (**www.canauthors.org**)
- The Canadian Publishers' Council (CPC) represents the interests of 30 companies that publish books and other media for elementary and secondary schools,

colleges and universities, and professional reference, retail and library markets. (Grossly simplified, the CPC represents the big publishers and the ACP represents the others.) (**www.pubcouncil.ca**)

- The Editors' Association of Canada (**www.editors.ca**), with branches across the country, offers regional referral "hotlines" for people needing editorial help.
- The Graphic Designers of Canada's website (**www.gdc.net**) has links to the sites of many of the association's members to help you find professional design help.
- The Indexing and Abstracting Society of Canada (**www.indexingsociety.ca**) has a referral service for anyone needing a book index prepared.

The next chapter guides you through the two preliminary steps in most publishing projects: preparing a budget and a schedule.

CHAPTER 3

ANALYSIS NOT PARALYSIS

There are two essential elements to virtually every publishing project: a budget and a schedule. This chapter leads you through the process of preparing both of these.

THE BUDGET

Publishing projects have a way of costing more that you dreamed possible. This chapter will help you anticipate and control your costs. Of course, if you are producing a photocopied, hand-bound book entirely by yourself, cost is not going to be a major consideration and you can skip this section. If you are independently wealthy, you can probably get by without a budget, too. (Of course, you didn't get to be independently wealthy by ignoring budget considerations!)

THE SCHEDULE

Do you need to produce your books by a certain date? If so, you need to prepare a schedule. Even if you have no "due date," you should have some idea of how long each step should take.

This chapter ends with a sample budget and schedule. But before we get to them, it is useful to consider the steps in the process individually, to look at how long they typically take and how they affect costs. The following estimate table shows what it would cost if you paid a professional to do each step and how long each step should take.

BUDGET AND SCHEDULE ESTIMATE

Step	Cost	Time	Comments
Prepare budget	nil	Varies	Don't get started publishing your book before you know what it will cost and how much revenue it will likely bring in.
Establish schedule	nil	Varies	The more hurried the schedule, the more things tend to cost.
Write first draft	30 cents per word	500 words per day	Most of the people reading this book have already written the manuscript. This discussion is just to put the work they've already done in context. Writing speeds vary widely. At 500 words a day, which is a rate that professional writers often quote, a 100,000-word manuscript takes 200 work days, or most of a year. And at 30 cents a word, the writer has earned $30,000 for that year's work. Writing is usually billed by the word, with rates ranging from about 20 cents a word to over $1 for corporate work and some magazine writing.

Step	Cost	Time	Comments
Obtain permissions	varies	varies	If you are printing something you didn't create, whether it is a portion of someone else's text or an illustration or photograph, you have to have the permission of the owner of the rights. Tracking down that owner and getting written permission can be extremely time-consuming. In many cases, you have to pay for the permission, which can become expensive very quickly.
Rewrite, if required	30 cents per word	500 words per day	Same comments as under writing. As a home publisher, you NEVER want to get into something as expensive as paying someone to rewrite your manuscript.
Edit for substance and structure	$25-$60 per hour	Varies from 100 to 1,500 words an hour.	Substantive editing is discussed in Chapter 4.
Edit for style	ditto	About 1,200 words an hour	Stylistic editing is discussed in Chapter 4.
Copyedit	ditto	About 1,500 words an hour	Copyediting is discussed in Chapter 4.
Title page, copyright page, cover copy	nil	One day	A whole batch of niggling little publishing chores that don't take long individually but can add up.
Index	$1,200 per 60,000 words is typical	10,000 words a day	See Chapter 5 for a discussion of indexing. The time it takes to prepare the index depends on the complexity of the book and how detailed an index is required.
Design	$300-$2,000	1 week	Includes front and back covers and internal design.

Step	Cost	Time	Comments
Layout	$4-$25 per page	Varies considerably	When you are getting quotes on layout, find out how long it should take.
Illustrations	$30-$500 each	Varies considerably	Discussed in Chapter 5.
Proofread first pages	$20-$50 an hour	1,500 to 3,000 words an hour	The proofreader is responsible for checking the work of the copy-editor and the layout person, so how quickly a book can be proof-read depends on how thoroughly it was edited and whether a professional layout person was used.
Check second pages	ditto	3,000 to 5,000 words an hour	
Check final pages	ditto	A few hours	
Check printer's proofs	ditto	A few hours	This check is often done at the printer's premises. It is the final step, just before the printer is ready to start the presses rolling. Making changes at this stage is extremely expensive.
Printing, paper and binding	Varies widely	One day to six weeks.	The time it takes to print and bind a book depends largely on the printing and binding methods used, and the quantity to be printed.
Promotion and sales	Varies widely	Varies widely	See Chapter 12

A SAMPLE BUDGET

The following budget tries to break even on selling 250 books. How realistic that sales target is really depends on the individual project. It is far better to set the projected sales as low as possible and get a pleasant surprise than to be too optimistic and lose a fortune.

TYPICAL HOME-PUBLISHING BUDGET:
a 128-page paperback with no interior illustrations

Expenses

Design	$300.00	A simple cover design and a prepackaged interior design template
Editing	$900.00	Copyediting only
Layout	$600.00	Following a very simple template
Proofreading	$400.00	One proofreading pass; you check that the corrections were done properly
Print 250 copies	$2,500.00	Printed offset; Cerlox bound
Contingency	$300.00	Some "just-in-case" money
Total Expenses	$5,000.00	
Cost per book	$10.00	

Income

Cover price	$20.00
Income from 250 sales	$5,000.00

FAMILY AND MONEY

We have already discussed how this project is indeed a labour of love. Although it may be true, it is also code for "don't expect to make a profit, unless you are related to King Tut." Your financial goal, if any, is to break even or at least to cover some of the costs of producing and shipping the book. The project's great reward will be finally seeing your family history documented and enjoyed by others for generations to come.

However gratifying this might be, you must consider how to pay for the book's production so you do not go into debt. Although money is the most contentious topic of discussion within families (apart from the topic of the cousin who ran away with the circus), you must deal with the financial realities. Three main courses of action are open to you.

Pay All Expenses Yourself

You can chose to produce a fairly inexpensive book with a small print run. Perhaps you feel that since you took on the project, you should shoulder the costs. Or, you are wealthy, generous and have no reservations about giving away hundreds of copies. If you can comfortably afford to take on all expenses involved in the book, you have no reason to worry about a potentially awkward conversation, or about what to give everyone for their birthdays next year.

Solicit Donations from Relatives

You are committed and passionate about the project, but you can't possibly pay for everything alone. How do you bring up the subject of a bit of financial help?

Some relatives, usually the ones who always remember your birthday, will offer you a donation without prompting.

With others, it might not occur to them to offer—it's all in the family after all. The best strategy is to let as many relatives as you can know in advance that you are writing this worthy book. Ask if those who can afford it would mind contributing a certain amount to help you cover the costs of printing and mailing out copies once it's finished. Casually mention that you would love to include colour photographs, but you're not sure if you can afford it. Once they understand that a small honorarium could enrich the project for the whole family, they'll probably be willing to help out.

Most people (yes, even people in your family) are very reasonable. They won't balk if you ask them to pay for the mailing costs, especially if they live in Malta.

Name Your Price

After you've sacrificed so much of your time, you realize you do need to charge for the book. To treat everyone fairly, you can simply sell the book to everyone for the same amount per copy. Determine what you think is a fair price based on your production costs (perhaps you hired an editor or a book designer), printing costs and shipping costs. You might forgo the charge if someone was particularly helpful with your research or lent you some great photographs. Even professional publishers give away a few complimentary copies when they must.

Of course, some relatives will expect to receive a copy for nothing. They feel you owe them for all the times they helped you move or babysat your temperamental poodle. How to deal with this situation is entirely in your hands. Each family has unique eccentricities, which is one reason telling their story is so worthwhile. It is best to bear in mind that this project commemorates your family's history and the bonds you share. Is it the time to squabble or the time to celebrate?

SAMPLE SCHEDULE

Most home-publishing ventures are done without any schedule in mind, which is as it should be. Most readers can skip straight to the beginning of Chapter 4. But, if you need your book to be finished by a particular date, such as the date of a family reunion, read on!

Schedules are prepared by counting backwards from the delivery date. To make this really explicit, this sample schedule is presented "upside-down," with the end-date in the first line.

Step	How long the step takes	Target date for completion of that step
Target date to have books in bookstores		September 1
Delivery to stores	1 week	August 24
Printing and binding	1 month	July 24
Indexing	2 days	July 22
Proofreading and correcting	1 week	July 15
Layout	1 week	July 7
Incorporating editor's suggestions	1 month	June 7
Editing	2 weeks	May 24
Design	1 week	May 17
Writing	6 months	November 17 (previous year)
Start date	—	June 17 (previous year)

This schedule is fairly typical. Of course, a schedule like this is only necessary when you have a definite target completion date. Early September is the most common target date in book publishing, because books published in the early fall benefit the most from the Christmas buying season (but it also means your book is competing for attention with all the bestsellers).

CHAPTER 4

PREPARING THE MANUSCRIPT

You've finally taken care of the biggest hurdle of all: you've written the manuscript. (Why are we skipping over the writing process? Because there are literally tens of thousands of books out there on the subject, and because we know that a considerable proportion of the readers of this book have already written their manuscripts.)

Before you start thinking that you are near the end of the process, be forewarned: as we have seen in that sample schedule, writing is only the first step in the long process of bringing a book to print.

This chapter explores the work that happens after the first draft is written: the notorious (and only sometimes painful) editing process.

PREPARING THE MANUSCRIPT

Book publishers expect manuscripts to be submitted in a specific format: single-sided, double spaced, 12-point type, and one-inch margins all around. There are various reasons for this. The standardized format (which has about 250 words a page) allows the publisher to estimate production costs very easily, and allows enough space for editorial corrections and comments.

Whether you as a self-publisher need to use that format depends on how the book will be produced. If it is going straight from your word processor to a desktop publisher, it really doesn't matter if you've strictly followed the format. If you intend to send it to a professional editor, the editor will probably be more comfortable working on the manuscript if it "looks right." Ask the editor; most editors are really put off by non-standard manuscripts, but some don't care.

When sending a manuscript to an editor or designer in the form of a computer file, the rule is really clear: "keep it simple." The editor or designer won't want lots of fancy fonts and pages that look like final layout. In most cases, they'll just have to undo the formatting before they start working on the file. So don't bother with the formatting unless the book is going to the printer right from your word-processed file.

HANDWRITTEN MANUSCRIPTS

At virtually every workshop for first-time writers and would-be home-publishers, someone asks: "Is it all right to submit handwritten manuscripts to editors or designers?" The answer is a resounding "no." There's not much that any of those people can do with a handwritten manuscript other than send it off to be keyed before they start working on it—and submitting something handwritten just looks extremely amateurish.

KNOWING WHEN TO STOP
TINKERING WITH THE MANUSCRIPT

There's no rule on when enough is enough. To a large extent, you'll have to rely on your own instincts. If you feel that you need help, trust that instinct. If you find that you've changed large parts of the manuscript back to how they had been in a previous draft, and are still not comfortable with them, get someone to help. If you're struggling with writer's block, or know that there is a problem with the manuscript but can't quite explain what it is (or just plain never want to see it again!) stop tinkering and get a friend or editor to look it over.

How Can an Editor Help You?

Anyone at all familiar with the publishing process will tell you that a skilled editor does much more than correct spelling mistakes. An editor is an organizer who rereads, revises, rearranges, reevaluates and, in some cases, rewrites an author's book. The editor is there to polish the manuscript and make sure it's fit to print. If you can afford a professional editor, that's the way to go. But if you're on a budget, you'll want to consider self-editing.

FREELANCE EDITORS

Most publishing companies use professional freelance editors to edit their books. If you have the budget, a freelancer can take on a variety of editing chores for you. Freelancers have widely varying levels of ability and fee schedules. If you want to have your book edited professionally, get at least two quotes on the work and be sure to get (and check!) references. To find freelancers in your area, contact the Editors' Association of Canada (see Chapter 2 under "Getting Help" for EAC website details), or look under "Editing" or "Publishing services" in your local *Yellow Pages*.

THE ART OF SELF-EDITING

Self-editing requires a great deal of objectivity and meticu-lousness (qualities that many otherwise detail-oriented people lack when confronted with their own writing). As a self-editor, you should be prepared to make many changes to your man-uscript before you complete a final draft, from the broadly conceptual cutting and pasting of structural editing to the technical refinement of the copyedit. The following pages out-line some basic components of each type of revision you will need to perform in order to make your self-published book the best it can be.

Keep in mind, however, that no one should be expected to write, edit and publish a book completely alone. It's a good idea to get some input from a potential reader before the book goes to press. If you want to publish a book that is engaging and error-free, give it to a friend or colleague you trust and ask for some objective feedback. But beware: most people are reluctant to criticize. You'll often have to grill the reader to find out what was really wrong with the manuscript. If you find yourself in serious disagreement with a friend's comments, give it to some-one else for a second opinion. Keep in mind that each person's sense about a piece of writing is subjective.

It's also important to remember that, when you ask a friend to read your work, you are requesting a favour. A surefire way to predispose people to dislike your work is to behave as though it were an honour that they should be "allowed" to read it.

What is Editing?

Editing includes making a manuscript logical, entertaining, clear and consistent. It is an extended process, with several stages:

Rewriting. It is often easier to give a manuscript with major problems a total rewrite rather than try to polish it. The rewriter uses the manuscript as a source of ideas and information, but writes the book again from scratch. Rewriting is EXPENSIVE! It typically takes six months to rewrite a book, so you can expect to pay the rewriter the equivalent of six months' salary.

Substantive or structural editing. If the material is reasonably well written but needs better organization or more clarification, it requires a structural edit (also called a substantive edit.) The editor reorganizes the manuscript, querying the author on gaps in logic.

Stylistic editing. The material is well organized, but there is too much jargon, or it is written for the wrong reading level. A stylistic editor "translates" the manuscript by smoothing out the language and tone.

Copyediting. What most people call "editing" is copyediting—fixing the grammar and spelling and watching for inconsistencies. This is also called "line editing."

Proofreading. A proofreader checks the work of the copyeditor and layout person. Many people mistakenly call the entire process "proofreading," but most proofreaders bridle at copyediting jobs disguised as proofreading. If it hasn't been copyedited, it isn't ready to be sent for proofreading!

For the self-editor, these stages will naturally overlap and merge as you embark on the path of revising your book. When looking for spelling errors, you will inevitably find yourself noticing organizational problems, and vice versa. Given this, the rest of this chapter is divided according to the basic principles at the heart of the editing process: rewriting, rearranging, stylistic editing, making the text correct and consistent and checking. And as for the cherry on top? There's also advice on how to come up with a knockout title.

Rewriting: Almost Back to Square One

The manuscript just plain doesn't work, and you don't know where to start fixing it. You really need help with it—but can't afford to hire someone for the months it will take. Where do you turn?

Many freelance editors are willing to do a manuscript evaluation. They don't actually edit the manuscript. Rather, they read it through and prepare a detailed memo outlining what works and what doesn't. They also offer suggestions on how to fix the problems they've pointed out. You end up doing most of the work yourself, but you are doing it with professional guidance— and you've paid someone for a few days of work, not a few months. The Writers' Union also offers a manuscript evaluation

---

MAKING IT ENTERTAINING

Maybe you have considered making your book strictly a genealogical study containing mostly charts, names and dates. But most manuscripts need to entertain their readers in order to keep them interested. You are writing a true story, the story of your family. Think of how wonderful it would be to enrich the facts with meaningful anecdotes and details that fit into a narrative. Fiction editors use a variety of "formulae" to make books entertaining. A formula is a standard "structure"—a way of organizing the information in the book. Here is one of the most common structures: You start with a fairly interesting incident to get the reader's attention, slowly build reader interest until the first climax, which comes about halfway through the book. That is followed by a section showing the consequences of the climax, with a slow, sustained buildup of tension

> until a more major climax at the end of the book. In other words, intro-
> duction> plot development> minor climax> more plot development>
> major climax> denouement. It works just as well for a family history as it
> does for a Harlequin.

service, as do the various writers in residence at universities, colleges and libraries. (See also the Writers in Electronic Residence
web page at **http://www.wier.ca**).

Rearranging: The Structural Edit

Not surprisingly, a structural edit involves reorganizing the
book to make sure it progresses logically from start to finish.
Rearranging can involve shifting entire episodes and sections
around, or cutting the manuscript up into its constituent paragraphs and shuffling them into a more logical—or entertaining—order.

A few questions to ask yourself at this is point are: Do my
thoughts follow in a logical order? Do I have all of the discussions of a single topic in the same place? Each of these factors
will contribute to the clarity and effect of your work as a whole.

Stylistic Editing

Paris Review: How much rewriting do you do?
Hemingway: It depends. I rewrote the ending to A Farewell To Arms,
the last page of it, thirty-nine times before I was satisfied.
*Paris Review: Was there some technical problem there? What had
stumped you?*
Hemingway: Getting the words right.

What Hemingway is calling rewriting is what we usually call
stylistic editing. He's not rethinking and starting again from
scratch—he is getting the words right. If you have all of the

pieces of your puzzle in the right place, but the result still feels clumsy, it's time to "restyle." Restyling is a way to even out the textual bumps and potholes that may have been introduced during restructuring. Now's the time to add details to liven up particular episodes, add the explanations the reader needs to follow your argument, get rid of those sentences you wrote in the passive voice or add in—or take out—that perfect adjective. Rewriting also involves carefully going over each line of your book to make sure that your meaning is not being obscured by awkward language, confusing jargon or clunky sentence structure.

But remember, the words you choose, and the order you place them in, constitute your own personal writing style. Stylistic editing is concerned with making a text more lively and readable, not more generic. During the self-editing process it is important to retain your particular, personal style.

~~MAKING THE TEXT SHORTER AND LESS VERBOSE~~
CONDENSING

Although it isn't unheard of for an author to underwrite, a far more common problem is overwriting. Extraneous details, trivial points or out-of-place digressions distract the reader and obscure the point you are attempting to bring across. Overwriting, whether in terms of style or just sheer length, can usually be fixed easily by some strategic cutting and tightening within the text. This process is often the most difficult part of the self-editing process. You must be objective enough to recognize when a word, sentence or whole section of your book is unnecessary.

Once the initial reduction work is complete, there are a number of questions self-editors must ask themselves upon re-reading their manuscripts, the most important of which is simply: Why? Why is this

> word/sentence/passage here? Why is it really necessary to the book as a whole? A careful editor must consider the worth of every paragraph, sentence and word in relation to the whole.

The most important part of stylistic editing is establishing and maintaining the author's voice. This applies to a family history, too. If, in an early chapter, you communicate in a conversational, jocular voice ("My mother always taught me that sweet roasted peppers are tastiest if you slather on lots of good olive oil."), you should make sure that this mode of expression is consistent throughout the book. If you later instruct the reader in a more formal tone ("My second cousin Joel instructed us in the application of viscous automotive lubricants."), you are using an inconsistent voice. Readers who have grown accustomed to your authorial voice will be jarred by any sudden shift in tone. This is your book, and your readers should be able to trust that it is the work of a single mind, unless, as in the case with this book, it is clearly presented as a collaboration.

Copyediting

Being your own copyeditor means paying attention to the technical aspects of your manuscript, rather than to content. In essence, copyediting involves checking grammar, spelling, punctuation and the general mechanics of style. At this stage you will also be checking for stylistic consistency within your book, as well as mapping out the placement of any graphics you are intending to use in the final product.

As your own copyeditor, you should make sure that the final text follows a uniform style. For instance, professional copyeditors will check that the text does not haphazardly jump from American to Canadian spelling. They'll also make sure that elements in the text have been given proper (and consistent) treatment: *italics* for foreign words (your prosperous Italian ancestors lived *la dolce vita*) or **bold** for special emphasis (perhaps for **April 9, 1955** at the top of each diary entry in a journal). Copyeditors usually draw up a "style sheet" that will give them a blueprint reference for the book's style. Creating your own style sheet and following it from start to finish is a handy reference when preforming the copyedit. If you're wondering whether to write "25" or "twenty-five" (and can't remember if you were only spelling out numbers below ten or one hundred), it's much easier to consult a style sheet than to flip back through the book and see what you've done elsewhere.

BOOKS ON STYLE

Many books will guide you through the intricacies of making your book stylistically consistent. Which one you choose will depend on what kind of book you intend to publish. Academic publishers usually rely on the *Chicago Manual of Style* (Chicago: University of Chicago Press). Trade publishers often use *Words Into Type* (Englewood Cliffs: Prentice Hall). An easy-to-understand introduction is the *New York Public Library Writer's Guide to Style and Usage* (New York: Harper Collins).

Careful copyediting will give your self-published project the same professional, polished look as a conventionally published book. It's also a way to ensure that your book is free of embarrassing mistakes, such as typos, before it goes to press.

Proofreading

Once you think the book's pages are finished—copyedited and laid out (layout is described in the next chapter) perfectly—it is time to bring in a proofreader, and preferably one who has never seen the book before. The proofreader is the final safety net. A good proofreader will catch and correct mistakes made by everyone in the process, and will make the corrections in such a way that your cost and inconvenience are minimized. Don't even consider proofreading the book yourself. You are far too close to it, and will miss virtually everything that is wrong.

SPELL CHEQUERS

Don't rely on a spell checker on your word-processor to catch all of your spelling mistakes. Their real bad at caching allsorts of miss steaks—such as the properly spelt "wrong" words in this box.

If you are having a friend proofread the book, make sure that person has everything necessary for the job: the copyeditor's style sheet and the style guide and dictionary that were used. Point out the things that caused special grief ("Watch for the correct spelling of a surname, such as Jonsson changed to Johnson after the family moved to Canada.").

Encourage the proofreader to ask lots of questions! Remember, this is the last person who is going to read the book all the way through before it is printed.

Finding a title

The last words you'll need to choose in the editorial process are the very first ones in the book: those that make up the title. Naming a book is not unlike naming a person—it needs to *feel* right, to fit the distinct personality of the work, and not just describe the contents. One need only imagine Salinger's *Catcher in the Rye* carrying the more literal title of *Holden Quits School*, or Shakespeare's *Twelfth Night* called *The Wonder Twins*, to realize the importance of choosing the right name for your book. Would

Woody Allen's acclaimed comedy *Annie Hall* have seemed as funny under its cumbersome original title, *Anhedonia*?

Ideally, a title will perform several essential functions in the relationship between a reader and your text. Not only should it name the topic of your book, a good title should also indicate the tone (whether humorous or sober), the voice (whether formal or chatty), and the literary style of your project. If you are planning to market your book, remember that you will rely on the title as much as the design of your book to attract the curious eyes and hands of bookshop browsers. It may be a good idea to scan a few bookshops yourself and make a list of the titles your own eye is naturally attracted to. You might want to consider a straightforward title, such as "The Yates Family," supplemented with a subtitle such as, "Our History in Canada since 1801."

It's a rare occurrence that a title reveals itself immediately. More often, an author uses a working title until a more catchy alternative jumps out of the text. It sometimes happens that the working title becomes a book's official title, but more often than not, a new title is required once the book is completely written and edited. A title should describe the contents of your book. That's the simple part. The hard part is choosing a name that, depending on the nature of your project, piques the interest of your intended reader. For instance, if your book is a family history aimed specifically at your personal family and friends, you'd be free to choose a title based on an inside family joke or reference. If, on the other hand, your book is meant to appeal to a wider audience, the book should correspondingly bear a more widely comprehensible title.

There are a number of techniques which will assist you in finding an engaging name for your work. One of the most tried and true ways of attracting a reader's attention is through the use of humour. A funny, resonant or just generally effective title can emerge in countless ways, some of which include:

- alliteration: as with, *Boom, Bust and Echo* and *Sense and Sensibility*;
- word play on well-known titles: as with, *A Book of One's Own* and *The Joy of Sex*;
- purposefully long titles: as with, *In Grand Central Station I Sat Down and Wept* and *You'll Never Eat Lunch in This Town Again*;
- direct, topical titles: as with, *How to Advertise* and *How to Make Friends and Influence People*; or
- the setting or main character as the title of the book: as with *Howard's End* or *Jane Eyre*.

Once you've stumbled across the perfect title, it's time to start thinking about bringing your manuscript to print. The next chapter will outline the basic preparations you need to convert your manuscript into a legitimate book.

CHAPTER 5

TO
DESIGN A
BOOK

Your manuscript is complete. You are satisfied that the editorial process is quite finished. You now move on to the next stage in the production life of a book: its design. What is your goal as you prepare to design your book? Producing an object of beauty? Creating a unique look? Finally being able to use some of those delightful typefaces that beckon from your font menu?

Put all these thoughts aside, because your primary goal in designing your book must be to make it easy to read. If you design a book that is illegible, nothing you have written and no fancy printing job can salvage it.

Your second goal in your role as designer is to make the book look interesting. You can do this by infusing the pages with variety while working within a consistent framework. This goal goes hand-in-hand with ease of reading.

When you find a design that accomplishes both of these objectives, you will have successfully designed your book and perhaps, in the process, created a uniquely beautiful work that uses just one of those tempting typefaces!

> ## WHAT YOU NEED TO KNOW ABOUT DESIGN OF THE HANDWRITTEN OR TYPEWRITTEN BOOK
>
> Good book design is not restricted to those who use a computer; the principles apply to handwritten and typewritten books, too. Even though writing or typing your book limits many of your choices, this can be a benefit when you're just getting started, because it can help you to focus on the overall appearance of the book instead of the niggling details that prevent you from seeing the "big picture." Continue to read this chapter to appreciate the role and function of book design—along the way you'll learn lots about how to make any kind of book you produce look and read better.

FINDING A BOOK DESIGNER

If you have the budget and you don't have an inclination toward design, or if your objective is to produce a lavish full-colour or hardcover book, you might want to hire a book designer. If this is the route you choose, you must look for a *book* designer. Any other kind of designer, whether they do print materials such as brochures, pamphlets, newspapers or catalogues, will not bring the book expertise that you need.

There are a number of ways to track down a book designer. Start with the design associations mentioned in Chapter 2, or you can look at an existing book for a design credit, and try to locate the designer. Just watch that the book you're looking at was produced in Canada; there's no sense in seeking a foreign supplier when many good designers are at work in this country. You can also check the reference book, *The Book Trade in Canada* (Toronto: Quill & Quire), in your local library; the Suppliers & Services chapter, Designers, Photographers & Production Services, provides some names. Finally, you can look under

Graphic Artists in your telephone directory. But, in this case, insist on someone with book experience, or it may be a case of the blind leading the blind.

Book designers charge a flat fee for their services; they are not paid a royalty. There will be one cost for the cover and one for the text. Just as printers need to know your printing plans, so too do designers. Before they can even quote on a job, they need to know the number of colours in which the text and cover will be printed. In general, a cover design fee will range between $300 and $1,000; text will cost another $200 to $1,000.

At the low end of the range, you get one design. At the high end, a designer will usually produce three rough designs—but be sure about what is included by asking up front. If you reject these designs, you may face an additional fee for the designer to keep trying. More often than not, if the first three designs don't produce a look you like, there is a communication problem between you and the designer. It will help to describe your intended audience for the book, and if you have sensitivities to certain images, share this information with the designer.

Book design is an art, not a science. Be open-minded to new ideas the designer might bring forward, but don't sacrifice your vision either. After all, it's your book and your money, so get what you want.

MIX IT UP

Maybe your budget doesn't allow you to invest in a professional design-er to do both the cover and the text, but you can afford one part or the other. A cover is more difficult to design successfully than text, so buy that service and provide the design for the text yourself. You'll be rewarded with a very professional-looking book at less cost.

THE DESIGN PROCESS

Whether you are handwriting the pages of your book, typing them or preparing them in a computer program, there is a logical series of elements to consider in the design process:

1. the look of the book: its overall tone, style, size and shape;
2. type: words on the page;
3. pictures: art, in all its forms, on the page;
4. pages: the combining of the words and pictures to create the book pages.

THE LOOK OF THE BOOK

It makes sense to begin the design process by matching the tone of the contents with a corresponding design. Just as there are different styles of writing, so too there are different styles of design. If your book is a straightforward genealogical study, then plan for your design to be conservative and traditional. If you're publishing a charming narrative history with many amusing anecdotes, your book should be friendly and playful in appearance.

At the end of this chapter you will find a Type Style Sheet which you can use to keep track of your design decisions. This will help you gather all the small choices into a cohesive whole when the time comes to begin making up pages. Your choice of style, then, will be your first entry on this form.

Also at the end of this chapter, you'll find another page where you can keep track of all your decisions regarding the elements of each page. Normally, we wouldn't encourage you to photocopy pages in a book, but for the Type Style Sheet and

Page Style Sheet, we'll make an exception. Make at least one copy of each so you'll have a working copy and then a final for your file. Keep the originals in this book clean for future use!

Your next design consideration is to identify the reading audience for the book. The reading audience can be different from the intended audience: Take a children's book that is meant to be read by a child. Its appearance will be quite different from a children's book that a parent will read to the child. Enter this information on the Type Style Sheet.

The overall style of the book is also determined by its size. A very distinct impression is made by a book that is very large, such as an art book, or very small, such as the tiny books often sold in stationers. Both are to be considered "precious," and you can see the extremes that publishers go to in order to create that impression!

Certain books are traditionally produced in certain sizes. It is unusual, for instance, to see a novel in an 8-1/2 x 11" size. Larger sizes, such as 8-1/2 x 11", are great for showing off illustrations, art and photographs, but they just aren't comfortable for people to hold for lengthy periods of reading. A minuscule book is a problem for the same reason: it's hard to read.

Therefore, if you are producing a family history in which many photographs will appear, lean toward a larger size, such as 8-1/2 x 11". If you are producing an illustrated children's book, 8 x 8" or 8 x 10" is good, because the pictures will be shown to their best advantage. All other types of books can be designed in the range of 6 x 9" for a professional look.

The final consideration in selecting the size for your book depends on whether you plan to print the book pages off your laser printer for saddlestitched binding. Please see page 97.

Take time now to decide on a size for your book. Enter this information on the Type Style Sheet. If you have trouble deciding, go to your bookshelf. Look at the books you like and think about whether your book would be appropriate in such a size. When in doubt, it is better to err on the conservative side.

The shape of a book is another important design consideration. There are three usual shapes:

- vertical, also called portrait;
- horizontal, also called landscape;
- square.

Vertical: Most books have a vertical shape—taller than they are wide—when closed. It is an easy shape to work with, and to hold while reading.

Horizontal: This type of book is bound on the short edge to create a book that is wide instead of tall and is most customarily used for children's books.

Square: Even though both height and width are equal, square books are always bound on the left edge of the closed book.

If you are at all unsure of which shape you want, choose vertical. Include your choice on your Type Style Sheet. At this point the big picture is complete—you will see your book beginning to take form. Now it is time to move to the particulars and bring life to the page.

ASSEMBLING THE PIECES ON YOUR COMPUTER

All of the words are finally in place. It is all written and edited. Now its appearance has to be polished a bit before it is ready to face the public. How you do the polishing depends on how complex the document is, and how it is to be printed.

Use a word processor if:

1. the book is simple, without a lot of sidebars, boxes, footnotes, etc.;
2. the book has few or no illustrations, photographs, and so on;
3. the printer can work with word-processor files or laser-printed output.

Use a layout program, such as Quark or InDesign, if:

1. the layout is complex;
2. the book is illustrated or uses colour;
3. the printer you choose asks for Quark or InDesign files or EPS files or a printout that has printers' marks.

Mac or PC?

"Mac versus PC" has reached the point of being a religious question rather than a debate over the comparative merits of two computer systems. One of the authors of this book swears by PCs, the other is a Macophile. The book-publishing world is similarly divided. Editorial departments tend to use PCs; design departments tend to use Macs. For the most part, that is the result of the history of the development of the software available for the two operating systems.

We're not going to agree about which is best, but we do agree that either computer system is perfectly capable of turning out books of any complexity. Almost all of the software discussed in this book is available for both platforms. Use whichever system you find comfortable.

If you choose a PC, be very wary of taking your book to printing companies where the staff know only how to use

Macs. Some printers will actually specify that files be delivered to them in a Mac format. If you use a Mac, follow the printer's instructions on formatting the Mac files. If you use a PC, there are plenty of PC-knowledgeable firms that will cause PC users far less grief than the Mac-only printers.

Word Processors

Microsoft Word dominates the word-processing market. It is wonderful for relatively simple documents, and can choke on complex documents. There are other word processors on the market, and some of these are very good at formatting text. The other word processors have such small market shares, alas, that it is difficult to find printers who can handle their files.

To design book pages in Word, you develop a template for your page layout grid, using different style tags for the different elements in the document. The style tags specify such things as font, margins, indent, spacing and other formatting factors. You then apply the template to your manuscript by going through the file and "tagging" each paragraph with the appropriate style.

That, at least, is how the programmers intend people to use the program. Many users don't use templates and style tagging, instead manually formatting the text as they go. That works well enough for short documents, but is a disastrous strategy for long documents. This is because, if you've formatted the document manually, you have to go through the entire document, tweaking the layout every time you change a design element. If you've used a template, changing a style in one place changes it throughout the document, so that the document maintains a consistent, professional feel. If you intend to prepare your finished pages using a word processor, take the time to learn how to use templates and styles before you start.

Once you feel the pages are print-ready and you want to secure the formatting, you can use software like Adobe Acrobat to convert your Word files into PDFs (portable document format). Be sure to have the program imbed the fonts into the document, so it will appear exactly the same on any computer and preserve the layout you have created when it goes to the printer. In newer versions of Acrobat, it is possible to do small edits (a word here or there) in a PDF, but if you want to make bigger changes, you'll have to go back to the original file.

Layout Programs

Layout programs offer far more control over the appearance of the book page than do word processors. They are also far more stable when working on complex designs or illustrations. For most book-publishing projects, it makes sense to use one of the major layout packages, which are available in PC or Mac formats.

There are several layout programs on the market designed for use with books. Although they can be difficult to learn at first, it might be worth the effort to design your book with software specifically made to work on very long documents. The two most-used layout programs, especially among professionals, are QuarkXPress and Adobe InDesign. Less popular programs, such as Corel Ventura, are also available.

Perhaps surprisingly, the layout programs use a concept that is rather similar to the "templates" found in word processors. They use "master pages." The design elements on the master pages, which you set up when you start, carry over to the individual book pages. You can import text from a word processor or type it directly into the layout you have created. As for photographs, you decide where to place them on the page and then import them from a separate file.

The biggest drawback to these programs is that they usually cost several hundred dollars. If you can't afford to spend that much, a good idea is to check auction websites such as **www.ebay.ca**, where you might find used copies of the software with original licences at less than the retail price.

Illustration Programs

Most industry professionals use Adobe Illustrator, but other less-popular programs such as Corel Draw are available. What they have in common is complexity: all of them are very difficult to use competently, and unless you are very familiar with one of them we would very strongly advise you to get a professional illustrator to prepare any computer-generated graphics for you.

Scanning and Photo Programs

Scanning art, photographs and documents is now very simple. Scanners come with software that will convert the scans into any of the common file formats such as GIFs, JPEGs or TIFFs. GIF (Graphic Image Format) files look fine on screen, but they display only 256 colours and the printed result looks dreadful. Don't use them for your book. The JPEG (developed by the Joint Photographic Experts Group) is often used for photos on the Internet and digital cameras. While it is a popular format, it does tend to degrade in quality each time the image is edited and resaved, so it's best not to change a JPEG too many times. TIFF (Tagged Image File Format) files preserve the quality of an image, but the files are large.

The usual problem with learning to scan is that beginners tend to use an unnecessarily high resolution and too large an image, so that the scanned files are gargantuan. However, scanning at too low a resolution could result in poor quality images. Resolution is measured in dpi (dots per inch), so the higher the number the more finely detailed the image. Generally, a scan for the inside of the book should be about 300 dpi at its original size. A scan for the cover, which you'll want to look great, might need to be as high res as 1200 dpi. Be sure to ask your printer what resolution to supply the scans in and what image file format is preferred. If you need high resolution scans for printing, you can make one set of low resolution scans for placing in your document and one set of high res scans on a separate CD, which you supply to the printer for placement in the files. This keeps your working file at a manageable size.

If you have a digital camera and you can take a photograph without decapitating your subjects, your own pictures could be a valuable addition to your book. Digital cameras are easy to use and you can download the images directly onto your computer. Although it's tempting to just point and shoot, read the camera's manual, experiment and learn all of its features to get the best quality images. As with a scanner, make sure to choose the right resolution, usually 300 dpi. Most cameras have a default setting of JPEG, but many also take TIFFs or RAW files. A RAW file is an unprocessed image, so you'll need to tweak it with photo editing software and convert it to a JPEG or TIFF. Editing a photo well is challenging; don't expect professional results immediately.

Although Photoshop (which can be a challenge to learn) is the most popular imaging program among professionals, there are less-complex programs that are much easier to use. Free photo editing software is also available on the Internet, such as Picasa 2 from Google.

DESKTOP PUBLISHING?

Desktop publishing was originally defined as using a PC or Mac operating system to create type and make-up pages instead of typesetting with specialized typesetting equipment. Now, virtually all type is created on screen (the desktop) and the term "desktop publishing" is used to describe a rather unprofessional-looking finished book. Obviously, after reading this book, your book will never suffer this fate!

Physical Manipulation, or How Do I Get There from Here?

You've planned your pages and you're ready to put the art or photos in place. How will you move from originals to copies?

To go on press, you will need to prepare an electronic file to send to the printer. If your files are too large to e-mail you can get them to the printer by FTP (File Transfer Protocol). Files are shrunk using file compression software, then transferred from your computer to an FTP site where the printer can download them. Certain Internet browsers (Explorer, Netscape) allow for FTP transfer, or you can download specific software. Also, the printer might still require a printout of your files along with the electronic copy, so speak with them to find out what types of files they accept and exactly how to proceed.

COLOUR ILLUSTRATIONS

If your art is in colour, but the text is black only, and you have access to a colour printer, you can print out your colour pages and manually insert them into the text pages. The problem here is that you will have produced an "insert" page that will not have text on the reverse. This is not very professional looking. The answer to this is called "tipping-in." To do this successfully, your colour piece should be smaller in dimensions than your page size. When the colour page is reproduced, there will be a white margin around the colour. Trim this off completely, and then apply two small dots of glue, such as rubber cement, to the wrong side of the two top corners of the art. Now position your colour art on the page. In effect, the book paper creates a frame around the art. This process can only be done after the pages have all been reproduced.

If you use high quality photo-grade paper to print the colour art or photos, you will have an excellent reproduction that can contribute enormously to the appearance of the book. You will, however, be producing each page from your printer, which could be a time-consuming process.

If you are not using a computer, take the originals to a copy shop where they can be photocopied and, in the process, enlarged or reduced. You will want one complete set of these copies made from all your originals. Then you can paste them onto your pages before they are once more either photocopied or actually printed. Unfortunately, quality will be sacrificed but this is still an inexpensive way of reproducing colour images.

TYPE

You could spend years studying the art of typography. It's a complete world, filled with its own language of ascenders, descenders, baselines and x-heights. But you don't need to know this language to choose the type form that is best for your book. What you do need to know is enough to get by to make a good set of decisions about type. Then you must exercise the discipline to carry those choices consistently through the entire book.

The Language of Type

A typeface refers to an entire family of letters of a design. Some well-known examples are Times Roman, Helvetica and Palatino. This book is set in Bembo.

There are five styles of type:

1. serif: lines project from each letter form: **T**
2. sans serif: sans means without; thus, without lines: **T**
3. script: letter forms simulate handwriting: *T*
4. decorative: letter forms are given a special treatment: T
5. special characters and symbols: special characters are created by a combination of key strokes. These characters create copyright, register and trade marks; currency symbols; and accents. Symbols, also called dingbats, wingdings or dingthings, do not produce letter forms but a combination of numbers and/or symbols. Musical notation is one example of a symbol face.

When selecting a typeface, don't be conned by those artistic "interesting" type styles. Stick to a serif face for the body text—they've been around forever because they are easy to read and beautiful as well. Look at which serif faces are available to you; choose one and insert this on your Type Style Sheet.

If you have chapter openings and/or subheads within the text, you can use an alternate form of the body text type or one that provides contrast. Please see the chart on the following page for some suggestions; once you've found a good candidate, include that on your Type Style Sheet too.

PICAS, POINTS, INCHES OR CENTIMETRES?

Typesetting has traditionally used picas and points as units of measurement, such as the example given for type size. Except for describing type size in points, we will use inches and centimetres as our unit of measurement on the basis that everyone has a ruler in these everyday measures. Rulers with picas and points are available through art supply shops.

Now more decisions await you regarding the typeface you've selected. Each of the following elements needs to be defined on your Type Style Sheet. Some of the entries on this form have been completed for you because sometimes there are simply no options but the normal, especially when dealing with body type.

Type size and leading: Size is the vertical measurement of a letter. Leading is the space between lines of type. Both elements are usually measured in points, i.e., 12/16 pt expresses type that is 12 pts in height with 16 pts of leading. Leading is usually described in word-processing programs as being a single line space, 1.5 line spaces or double line spaces.

Weight: The density of the letters can be anywhere from light to extra bold.

Width: The horizontal measurement of a letter is described as condensed, normal or expanded.

Slant: The angle of a letter encompasses both roman (vertical) and italic (oblique) forms.

Style: The options applied to type include underlining, strikethrough, superscript, subscript, shadow, reverse and outline.

Case: Letters can be capitalized in different ways. They can be either upper and lower case, small caps or uppercase (all caps).

The Conventions of Type

To the amateur typesetter there can seem to be an almost overwhelming number of choices to make about type. Luckily there are certain rules that can make the process a lot easier:

- Don't ever use a type size for body text that is smaller than 10 pts (what you would customarily see in a business letter) or larger than 16 pts (an extra large children's fairy tale book, for instance).

- Don't scrimp on leading, but don't go overboard either. Generous leading invites legibility, but too much can look silly. Strike a balance between too little and too much. Usually 10 pt type is well balanced by 12 pt leading, 12 pt type with 14 pt leading, 14 pt type with 16 leading and 16 pt type with 18 leading.
- Make the line length proportional to the page size and dimension. If you are producing a book that is horizontal in shape, it can support longer lines. The longer the line, the larger the type. A line length should never exceed 5", and closer to 4" is optimal. Maintain wide margins all around.
- Use roman face for text.
- Use **bold** face to create emphasis.
- Use *italic* face for captions and quotes that repeat text from other sources.
- Use ALL CAPS for short "headlines" such as chapter titles; otherwise do not use all caps as a type treatment.

FORMATTING TIPS

Proper formatting of the text will produce a professional-looking book. Here are some tips that will make a big difference in the look of your book.

1. Insert only one space after punctuation: the good old double space at the end of a sentence is not used in typography.
2. Create proper dashes: instead of two or three hyphens, use an en-dash (-) or an em-dash (—).
   En-dashes are created by:
   Mac: space option hyphen space
   PC: ctrl =

Em-dashes are created by:

Mac: option shift hyphen

PC (Word): hold down the ctrl, alt, and numlock keys

and press the minus sign in the number pad

3. Create true quotation marks by:

Double quotes: Mac: option [to open

option shift [to close

PC: Select the SmartQuotes option and

quotes will be styled automatically

Single quotes: Mac: option] to open

option shift] to close

PC: Select the SmartQuotes option and

quotes will be styled automatically

4. Paragraphs that follow a head are called lead paragraphs. Don't indent them.

To make these changes throughout your manuscript, use the find-and-replace option for the double spaces, hyphens and quotes. Lead paragraph indents will have to be manually removed.

TYPE IN COLOUR

Why do you want type in colour? To create interest? To make the book look snazzy? To impress your family?

Unless you are going to make the type all one colour instead of black, give it up! If any of the above reasons are your objective, go back and revisit your type specs, or (dare we say it?) your content. Type in colour is best left to the gifted typographic artists and the pros.

If you are looking for one colour other than black, it must have enough tone to provide sufficient contrast with the paper or the words will be lost on the page. So, you can use a dark-toned blue, brown or green, but given the fidgeting required to pull it off successfully, it's just not recommended.

WHAT MAKES A BOOK?

There are three basic sections to a book. They are the preliminary pages, body and end matter. Not all books have end matter, and some are very light in the prelims, but they all have a body.

PRELIMINARY PAGES

The prelims include the half-title (if you are using one), title, copyright, contents, acknowledgments and foreword. These pages will be created singly and therefore designed individually.

While you must obviously work within the parameters of your page, there are no hard and fast rules for the design and make up of these pages. Let aesthetics be your guide, and design them to please the eye. Use common sense and remember your design objectives of legibility and interest.

Create a separate file for this portion of the book. When you have made a first pass to capture the information, save the file and back it up.

What goes where:

Half-title. If you are putting in a half-title, it will be the very first page in the book. This page is not necessary. The only type on the half-title is the title of the book. Quite often, the book title will appear in the same face as it does on the front cover, though it is usually smaller.

The back of the half-title is blank.

Title. The title page includes the title, subtitle, author's name and name and logo of the publisher. As with the half-title, the title and subtitle are often adapted from the front cover.

The back of the title page is the copyright page.

Copyright page. The copyright page contains all the legal stuff: copyright notice, rights notice, name and address of publisher, ISBN and the library catalogue notice (CIP). In setting this page, you may find you have a lot to fit in a relatively small space. This is one of two places in the book where you may have to make your type size considerably smaller than elsewhere; the other is the index. Also, if you set this type smaller, this page will become less conspicuous than it otherwise might be.

The next page is usually the *table of contents*. If it is longer than one page, it will run onto the back of that page. Otherwise the back will be a blank. You will not be able to insert your page numbers on the contents page until the book is finalized. Follow convention in the creation of these pages. They are really just a buildup to the main event: page one!

PAGE 1 OR PAGE i?

Usually if the preliminary pages are numbered, roman numerals are used. Then the first text page is page 1. However, sometimes the very first page in the book is treated as page 1. The latter treatment makes it look as if there are more pages in the book, and helps to justify those high prices!

PAGE ONE AND ON: THE TEXT

This is what you've been waiting for: the chance to make a book starting with the first words of your manuscript.

The easiest way to create pages is to develop a grid. A grid is simply a structure for the type that is applied consistently across the pages. The beauty of using a grid is that many of your decisions regarding page composition are made once: when you design the grid. Without a grid, each page could be a nightmarish trial-and-error process and the book a mishmash.

A grid for book pages is different from other printed materials in that the type on a book page is usually formed in one wide column. Newspapers, magazines, newsletters and, occasionally, books that are wider than they are high, are formatted into multi-column grids. The longer line length of type on a book page brings a different set of design requirements than do other print materials.

The text pages are composed of the body (the story, if you will), with a running head that usually gives the title of the book on the left page and the chapter title on the right, and a page number (also called a folio) with each of them. When a new chapter begins, there is usually some combination of chapter number and name.

QUITE EXCEPTIONAL!

Of course, just as one establishes a set of rules or guidelines to try to simplify the book-making process, the exceptions start popping up. Bear these tips in mind for the most professional look in page design:

- Chapter openings don't have running heads.
- Picture pages on which a single image is featured don't need page numbers or running heads; sometimes, for the biggest impact, even the caption is placed on the facing text page.
- Preliminary pages usually don't have page numbers or running heads.
- End matter pages (bibliographies, indexes, etc.) usually have page numbers and running heads.

Just as you had to make decisions regarding the type itself, so too you must decide how and where to put the type within the grid. This is called alignment. Alignment describes how lines of type align on the page: left margin type aligns on the left margin, justified type aligns on both margins, centred type lines up down the centre of the page and right margin type lines up on the right margin.

Although most books have justified type, trying to justify the text can become a nightmare if you are using a word processor. You can end up with large spaces between words or even letters. If this happens, it is best to abandon justification and line up the text on the left margin.

Good applications for the alignment options are listed below:

Left margin: most books, including family histories, use this traditional alignment for the narrative portions

Centred: use this if you've included interesting or unusual bits such as poetry or family recipes

Right margin: if your book contains old photos, artwork or other illustrative elements, you will use this alignment for the captions

You can also use different forms of alignment for different elements within a book. An old family recipe, for instance, might have the recipe title and ingredients list set in a centred format, but the cooking instructions would be set starting on the left margin of the page.

GRIDS

There are three kinds of grids, but only two that are recommended for the home publisher: either the minimum or the simple grid. The professional grid is discussed briefly, but its execution requires a grasp of so many variables that its use is better left to the design experts.

The Minimum Grid

This grid is used for books that don't have page numbers, running heads or, usually, chapter titles. It only delineates margins indicating where the story should be placed on the page.

The Simple Grid

The most simple grid doesn't distinguish between left- and right-hand pages. This means:

- equal margins on the left and right
- page numbers, chapter opening titles and running heads that are centred

Such a grid can be used for any kind of book. It is easy to work with and can be easily and quickly set up on your word processor. This grid is best for books of 60 or fewer pages in length; longer books will tend to look tedious. For a longer book, monotony can be avoided by introducing levels of subheads in the text in order to break up large text blocks; or using art—either illustrations, photographs or technical art such as maps, charts and diagrams; and/or by using a second colour for some of the type.

The Professional Grid

This kind of grid is the trickiest to work with because the left- and right-hand pages are treated differently:

- The margin may or may not be equal on each side of the page.

- Page numbers and running heads are positioned on the left- or right-hand margins.
- The text type is usually justified.
- Chapter opening titles can be centred or not.

There's a lot of information to plan and track as the pages are assembled. To avoid frustration, this kind of grid should only be attempted after one of the easier grids has been used.

Making a Grid

You will have two options when it comes to making a grid: you can make your own, or you can use or adapt one of the grids you'll find in the Appendix, starting on page 141.

To make your own grid, you must enter all your decisions about how the pages will be formatted onto the Page Style Sheet, which is provided on pages 74 and 75. Just as the Type Style Sheet is your record of type decisions, the Page Style Sheet is how you will remember what you decided about how the pages will look.

When you have made all the necessary choices, it is a good idea to make yourself a "dummy" page:

- cut a piece of paper the size of the finished book
- pencil in the box where the text type will appear on the page
- draw a line to represent the running head and a capital X for the page number
- if there will be photos, draw a box to represent where the photo will be placed on the page, and lines to show the caption (if using)

Now, take a good hard look at what you've designed. Is there lots of space for the margins and between the type elements?

Does it look like these pages are going to be easy to read? If not, keep trying by looking at other books until you arrive at a design that works.

The other way of developing a grid is to use one that is provided in the following pages. Even if you want to work up your own, seeing how the professionals do it will give you ideas and direction.

Once you're satisfied with your grid, set the parameters for margins, alignment, page numbers and running heads (also called headers) in your computer file in which you are making the pages. Then you must resolve to stick with it no matter how tempted you are to make exceptions!

END MATTER

End matter consists of the index, bibliography or other aspects of the book that are rightly placed at its end. If you have many pages that classify as end matter, you will want to create a grid; otherwise, if there is only a page or two, a grid is not required. Use good design sense to make sure the pages are legible and maintain the same margins as in the text pages.

PICTURES ON THE PAGE

If you plan to include any kind of pictures in your book, this section is for you. If you're not, skip ahead to the details on making up pages, page 68.

A wide variety of illustrations might appear in your book. There are photographs, art, documents (such as birth certificates, marriage licenses) and maps, lists, tables and graphs. We'll use the words "photos" or "art" to mean any illustrative element.

While books that include illustrations always look more interesting than those without, this interest is created and sustained only if the art meets certain requirements. You should ask the following questions when selecting art for inclusion:

Does the art match the style of the book?

Just as you match type to the tone of the book, so, too, must illustrations be a good fit. Cartoons are great in a kid's book, but they are risky in your family history.

Can I change the tone of the book with art?

Yes, if you're very careful. Editorial cartoons, for instance, address very serious subjects using a lighthearted approach. You can try the same technique of using cartoons to enliven your book, for instance. But be sensitive and err on the side of caution. Don't forget to ask for and receive permission from the artist or publisher before using art that appears elsewhere.

Is the piece of art technically sound?

Photographs must be in focus. They also need sufficient contrast to be easily discernible. Photographs of people must be at close enough range to see the faces.

Documents, charts and other technical art should be chosen with legibility in mind.

Is the artwork aesthetically sound?

Children's drawings can be charmingly naive, but will they appear so to anyone but the parents of the artist? Take a tough stand on this, even if you are the parent.

Photographs that are "negative" in mood or content tend to create a very negative reaction in the viewer. Many people feel that a photograph of something that's ugly can be

ILLUSTRATIONS

During your tireless hours of research, you have collected remarkable odds and ends. Illustrative elements make the book look like a true work of art, and they make the story come to life with historical authenticity. Think beyond your carefully planned charts and wonderful photographs; the variety of items you can include is limitless. Your local genealogical society can offer suggestions and examples, as well as advice on where to find some unusual pieces.

Interesting or relevant newspaper clippings put your family's story into a greater context. A small-town newspaper clipping about your great-grandfather and his prize-winning goat would be enjoyed by anyone reading your book. Check the archives of your local library.

Copies of old, handwritten letters or journal entries provide an understanding of the lives of your relatives. Just make sure you have permission to use them, and leave out anything that could be embarrassing or too personal. Resist the temptation to include steamy love letters.

Poems or short bits of prose written by your great-grandmother, for example, would be fascinating to share with others. Consider this option if it really enhances the book, don't just use it as an excuse to publish your six-year-old's poems about a mouse and its house, no matter how precious.

If a great-uncle owned a restaurant, is there a copy of the original menu? Has anyone saved a ticket stub from a well-known event? Ask your relatives as you research. You'll be amazed at the kinds of mementos they'll have.

really instructive, because they think it can show you what not to do. Forget about taking that approach. Show the very best—or the most beautiful—picture you can to make your point.

Does the art correlate with and contribute to the text?

If the art—whether it's a photo, drawing, or chart—has no bearing on the text, it shouldn't be included.

Is it in good taste?

No, you can't be the arbiter of tastefulness to one and all. But if the photo or art in question will cause embarrassment to others, or if it qualifies as being questionable, do yourself a favour and keep it in your private collection.

Is it kind?

This is not a technique issue, but one to bear in mind in any case. By way of example let's say your child has produced an amazing portrait of her grandmother that shows a lovely smile, twinkling blue eyes, silvery gray hair—and the large wart on the side of her nose. Must you really preserve this for posterity? The same goes for photographs: if you have a choice, try for the flattering view.

WHERE TO PUT THE PICTURES ON THE PAGES

Pictures can be placed on the same pages on which text appears, on their own page, or in sections, to create the feel of a "photo album."

On the Page

If a photo and text are to be integrated on the same page, then the best—and easiest to manage—position for the photo is at the bottom of the page. In this case, the space the photo occupies on the page simply replaces space the text would have used. The photo does not go into the margin. However, this can quickly become rather tedious-looking. A good way to alleviate this problem is to occasionally insert full-page photo pages. The page facing the chapter opening is a good place to do this.

Photos on Their Own

In this case, the photo will be on its own on the page. When a photo or piece of art is treated this way, it should be confined within a wide margin or "bleed" right off the page (see page 123 for a discussion about bleed). Each photo should be the same size on the page.

Photo Sections

Sometimes photos comprise their own section in a book and create the feel of a photo album. Multiple images, in different shapes and sizes, can be incorporated to be visually appealing. Such sections are usually not less than four pages each within the book; there may be any number of such sections.

Captions

Captions need to accompany almost all photos, documents and other art forms. If at all possible, the caption should be informative, and not just repeat facts in the text. For instance, instead of simply stating the name of the person in a portrait, you could add a tidbit filling in details about the person. So "Lyla Buttle" would become "Lyla Buttle, founder of the mining community of Hailey's Station."

The type for captions should be one size smaller than the body text, and the leading should be tighter. An italic typeface is a handsome choice.

THE METHOD FOR MAKE UP

With your grid in place, you can then proceed to "make up" pages. This is also known as layout. It is a methodical process that requires patience; don't try to take shortcuts! Do things properly at this stage and you'll avoid future headaches.

Depending on what program you are using you will either import or cut and paste the text onto the grid page(s) you've created. If you keep the book in one file, the computer keeps track of which pages fall on the left and which fall on the right; the disadvantage is that you might have quite a large file to work with.

If you're not using a computer, you'll still want to follow the grid you've developed to ensure consistency across all the book pages. Take the paper that will become your book pages and lightly mark on each piece the guidelines you'll need to follow to place your text correctly. Faint pencil marks can always be erased later. Then, either write your manuscript in the text block space or cut and paste typewritten pages to fit within the guidelines.

Start page one on a right hand page and then let the text flow from there. Make sure you start new chapters on a new page but otherwise don't worry about fiddling with awkward word and line breaks; you want to get all the manuscript moved onto grid pages before starting the fancy stuff.

Once you've got this step accomplished, make a backup of your file on a floppy disk, CD or some external means such as an FTP site.

Then go back to page one and start to apply your type styles. Apply each type style according to the decisions you made on your Type Style Sheet. Use your program's "Style" function. If necessary, learn how to use this to create the typography you have designed.

Make sure that you have tested your chosen typefaces before running through the entire book. Some fonts appear on the computer screen only and will not print. A quick check to make sure everything works, and looks, the way it is supposed to can save a lot of time.

Work on every page and every element of each page in sequence: don't jump back and forth. Treat chapter openings as you come upon them and deal with any "exceptions" as they arise. When you've finished, back this up.

This is now a good time to print out all the pages on paper. You will be surprised at the number of mistakes, inconsistencies, typos and omissions that will jump out at you from the paper that you just couldn't see on the computer screen. Read the pages carefully, and be sure that you're happy with the look you've created. It's not too late to go back in and make changes, but make sure you understand your rationale for such change. When this line-by-line, page-by-page review is completed, go back to page one in your layout and work your way through the book, fixing all the problems you've identified.

There will be two problems that you are certain to see when you look at these pages: poor hyphenation and what are called "widows" and "orphans."

Hyphenation. When a word fails to hyphenate, you can have a very large space on the end of a line. Such spaces disrupt the flow of reading and look ugly. Use your program's hyphenation function. You may also find words that have failed to hyphenate correctly; these must be fixed manually. If you're in doubt as to the correct way to hyphenate a word, use your dictionary. Finally some words may hyphenate correctly, but their hyphenated form is unconventional. For instance a line beginning with "ly" just looks bad. These, too, should be fixed.

Never begin a line with a dash or hyphen; if either starts on the left margin, force it onto the end of the line above or bring down a word to precede it.

Widows/orphans. Sometimes you will see at the top of a page the last line or two, or even just a few words, of the preceding paragraph. A single word or line of type ending a paragraph and left to dangle at the top of the next page or column is a widow. Similarly, an orphan is a single line of type that begins a new paragraph at the bottom of a column or page. These lines or words look lonely, and in fact that's exactly how they are corrected: by giving them some company. If you need to add lines on a left-hand page, decrease the number of lines on the preceding two pages by one each and add these two lines to your widow. If you need to add lines on a right-hand page, decrease the number of lines on the page before and the preceding two pages by one each and add these three lines to your widow. If it's just a word or two, see if you can force it back onto the preceding page by some judicious editing. If this isn't possible, force lines to come forward. Most programs do this automatically.

It is quite possible in fixing some problems to create others. As you make changes, keep an eye out for what is happening to the lines above and below where you're working. Scan each page before going to the next. Finally, back it up and print it out again. This is your final check. At this point you'll have page numbers in place. This allows you to go back and complete your table of contents to finish up the preliminary pages, and to write your index.

If you're going to press with the book, when the pages are finished to your satisfaction, you'll need to provide your printing company with the materials from which they will make the

WRITING AN INDEX

An index is essential in all non-fiction works for one good reason: it lets people find information easily and without guesswork. Computer word-processing programs with a sort function have made the creation of proper-name indexes a breeze. The best source of information about how to write the index is found in *The Chicago Manual of Style* (Chicago: University of Chicago Press).

film that produces the printing plates. If you're providing everything on disk, make sure it's in a format they can use. It's a good idea to make a small sample disk before the project is completed to ensure compatibility between your system and theirs. Always include a paper-copy print-out of the text. It is an important reference for the person who will do the manipulation of the files.

If you're providing the pages on paper, called camera-ready art, each page will need to be printed on the highest quality white stock. If photographs or illustrations form part of the book, each one will have to be identified as to where it goes, as well as its size. A photograph that is to be printed in its original size would be indicated to print—this is called "sized at"—100%; a picture that is to be half as large as the original you're supplying would be sized at 50%; twice as large would be 200% and so on.

If any of these steps cause difficulty for you, ask the printer of the job for help. Communication with the pros can save you time, energy and money.

TYPE STYLE SHEET

Use this sheet as you read through this chapter to keep track of the decisions you make about design and type.

1. The style that best suits the content for my book is:

O conservative   O serious   O elegant

O friendly   O playful   O lively

O stylish   O sophisticated   O trendy

2. The size of the finished book will be: (insert measurement)

_____ (height) x _____ (width)

3. shape: O vertical   O horizontal   O square

4. Type specifications:

text:

typeface: _____

type size and leading: _____

weight: _____

width: normal

slant: roman

style: not applicable

case: upper and lower case

chapter openings:

typeface: _____

type size and leading: _____

weight: _____

width: _____

slant: _____

style: _____

case: _____

subheads:

typeface: _____

type size and leading: _____

weight: _____

width: _____

slant: _____

style: _____

case: _____

(If there are heads, subheads and then more subheads, keep track of their number and type specs on this sheet.)

photo captions:

typeface: _____

type size and leading: _____

weight: _____

width: _____

slant: _____

style: not applicable

case: upper and lower case

running heads:

typeface: _____

type size: _____

weight: _____

width: _____

slant: _____

style: not applicable

case: upper and lower case

PAGE STYLE SHEET

Use this sheet as you read through this chapter to keep track of the decisions you make about page format.

1. complexity of grid:　　○ minimum (go to 2)

　　　　　　　　　　　　　　○ simple (go to 3)

　　　　　　　　　　　　　　○ professional (go to 4)

2. minimum grid: text pages:

margins: (insert measurement)　　left: _____ right: _____

　　　　　　　　　　　　　　　　top: _____ bottom: _____

type alignment:　○ left margin　○ justified　　○ centred

3. simple grid: text pages:

margins: (insert measurement)　　left: _____ right: _____

　　　　　　　　　　　　　　　　top: _____ bottom: _____

type alignment:　○ left margin　○ justified　　○ centred

page number:　　○ top of page　○ bottom of page

　　　　　　　　○ left margin　　○ centred　　　○ right margin

running head:　　○ no ○ yes:　○ centred　　　○ left margin

4. professional grid: left-hand text pages

margins: (insert measurement)　　left: _____ right: _____

　　　　　　　　　　　　　　　　top: _____ bottom: _____

type alignment:　○ left margin　○ justified　　○ centred

page number:　　○ top of page　○ bottom of page

　　　　　　　　○ left margin　　○ centred

running head:　　○ no ○ yes:　○ centred　　　○ left margin

professional grid: right-hand text pages

margins: (insert measurement)　　left: _____ right: _____

　　　　　　　　　　　　　　　　top: _____ bottom: _____

type alignment:　○ left margin　○ justified　　○ centred

page number:　　○ top of page　○ bottom of page

　　　　　　　　○ centred　　　○ right margin

running head:　　○ no ○ yes:　○ centred　　　○ left margin

5. Does the book have chapters? If yes, chapter opening pages:

margin: (insert measurement from top edge of finished book page to line on which chapter title/number will be placed) top: _____

type alignment: ○ left margin   ○ centred   ○ right margin

page number: ○ bottom of page

               ○ left margin   ○ centred   ○ right margin

running head: ○ no

6. Does the book have pictures? If yes, pictures will appear:

           ○ with text (go to 7)

           ○ on their own pages (go to 8)

           ○ in photo sections (go to 9)

7. Pictures in text need:

margins around pictures: left: _____ right: _____

(insert measurement)   top: _____ bottom: _____

captions: ○ yes   ○ no

8. Picture pages need:

margins around pictures: left: _____ right: _____

(insert measurement)   top: _____ bottom: _____

captions: ○ yes   ○ no

page number: ○ no

running head: ○ no

9. Photo section pages need:

margins around pictures: left: _____ right: _____

(insert measurement)   top: _____ bottom: _____

captions: ○ yes

page number: ○ top of page   ○ bottom of page

               ○ left margin   ○ centred   ○ right margin

running head: ○ yes   ○ no

GOOD TYPE CHOICES FOR YOUR BOOK

Here are some very standard typefaces that are pleasing to the eye. Mix and match at your own peril!

CLASSIC

Chapter One

Roots in Limerick

James was born in Cork in 1756. He apprenticed to a weaver of linen at the age of 12. When he was 18, he left Cork and went to work in a weaver's shop in Limerick, which was a long way to travel in those days.

Heading One: Times, 48 pt
Heading Two: Times Bold, 16 pt
Text: Times, 12/16

MODERN

Chapter 1

Roots in Limerick

James was born in Cork in 1756. He apprenticed to a weaver of linen at the age of 12. When he was 18, he left Cork and went to work in a weaver's shop in Limerick, which was a long way to travel in those days.

Heading One: Rotis SemiSans, Extra Bold, 48 pt
Heading Two: Rotis SemiSerif, Bold, 16 pt
Text: Rotis Serif, 11/14

ELEGANT

CHAPTER ONE

Roots in Limerick

James was born in Cork in 1756. He apprenticed to a weaver of linen at the age of 12. When he was 18, he left Cork and went to work in a weaver's shop in Limerick, which was a long way to travel in those days.

Heading One: Trajan, 24 pt
Heading Two: Bembo Bold, 12 pt
Text: Bembo, 11/14

CHAPTER 6

WRITING AND DESIGNING A COVER THAT WORKS

Can you tell a book by its cover? One thing is for sure: even though a cover can't give you the complete story about what's on the inside, the cover does tell a lot about the book. Beyond the title and the author's name, it establishes a style, or tone, for the book.

Since personal preferences vary wildly, it can be somewhat difficult to pin down exactly what makes a great cover, but it's very easy to identify what makes a bad one. Think about the dreadful covers you've seen: the ones that are hard to read, the ones that use a depressing colour or ugly image, the ones that look like a high-school yearbook. All of these tend to be very effective in creating one response in the beholder: the avoidance response!

You can learn a lot from this. You can learn that you want your book to attract attention and to be welcomed by its readers.

The sheer number of great cover designs out there proves that this can be easily accomplished.

COVER vs JACKET

You will determine in Chapter 10 whether you are making a cover or a jacket. But let's quickly summerize: a **cover** is the heavy printed paper encasing the pages of a softcover book, while a **jacket** wraps around the case of a hardcover book. You will probably choose to produce a softcover book. Either way, you'll want the outside of the book to be beautiful.

THE BASICS

Your book **cover** should include:

	At the Minimum	The Maximum
Front	• title	• title
		• subtitle
	• author's name	• author's name
Spine	• title	• title
	• author's surname	• author's surname or whole name
		• logo of publisher
		• publisher's name
Back	• nothing	• title
		• subtitle
		• back cover copy
		• price
		• ISBN
		• bar code
		• author's credentials

If you're producing a jacket, you have the luxury of the flaps to give the reader all the important selling information. The front jacket flap is used for a repeat of the book title, the price and copy that briefly describes the book. The back flap is used for the author's credentials, often an author photograph, a credit line for the photograph of the author, and the publisher's name. Quite often the jacket back only includes an illustration with the ISBN and bar code.

THE FRONT COVER

Since the importance of the front cover is pretty much established, you have good motivation to make yours the best it can be. There are five no-fail rules for good cover design:

1. Keep the design simple.
2. Don't attempt too much colour.
3. Ensure that whatever photograph or illustration you choose to use is of excellent quality.
4. Choose a cover treatment that's appropriate for the subject or nature of the book.
5. If it doesn't work, throw it out and start over.

ADOPT AND ADAPT

It's no crime to find a cover you love on an existing book and adapt its design for your own book. It won't violate the copyright on the published work as long as you do not exactly reproduce the other cover—including its title! You will probably find it much easier to design a cover by mimicking the typeface and style combined with the sort of illustration that appears on the cover you admire and apply your personal adjustments. In the end, these individualized flourishes will make it your own.

RULE ONE: Simplicity

The structure of a front cover is straightforward: the title usually appears in the top third of the cover, and the author's name in the bottom third.

So let us assume that you have chosen a great title based on the advice on page 37. Now you must consider fit and legibility. The title has to fit in the space you have available. A title that is too long can create legibility problems. A title that is too short can be meaningless to everyone except its author.

Legibility problems can be created by:

- type that's too small
- type that's too large
- inappropriate typefaces
- type that is printed over an illustration or photograph

The solutions to the first three of these problems are obvious: pick a type size that is large enough to be read easily without being overpowering, don't allow words to hyphenate and don't use fancy typefaces—usually a good standard font like Times is all you need. Avoid script typefaces. Script type is best saved for wedding invitations; no one will be fooled into thinking the cover is handwritten if you use a script face.

Setting type over an illustration, photograph or art of any kind is usually best left to a design expert. It is perfectly acceptable to produce a book cover that does not include any illustrative element. However, if you do build in an illustration or photograph, plan to position your type above the illustration, beside it or below it. Type that runs over top of an illustration can quickly become illegible.

SIMPLICITY IS THE SECRET

A busy cover design is a telltale sign of a self-published book. Remember, the cover doesn't have to tell the whole story—that's what you've got the text pages for. Make your cover easy to read and good to look at.

RULE TWO: Don't Attempt Too Much

Writing a book is quite an accomplishment; expecting to design it so well that you can quit your day job and join the ranks of book designers may be somewhat unrealistic. See Rule One: Keep your use of title, type and layout simple.

Be careful with colour. Remember that without sufficient contrast between the background and the type, the type can't be read. And just as colours connote meanings in other areas of life, so do they in books: dark blues and purples convey richness and authority; black is dramatic and sombre; white is clean and eye-catching; greens are fresh; reds, oranges and yellows are hot! Don't even think about brown. Publishers believe that brown books don't sell, and as a consequence you will not see many brown books on the shelves. (You'll notice that this book is...sort-of brown.)

BLACK COVERS

Warning about black: It might look wonderful as a background cover colour but it is more subject to scuffing—rub marks—than any other shade. Once scuffed, the book looks badly used.

RULE THREE: Illustration

You have decided to include a photograph in the centre of the front cover. Let us hope in this case that you own the photo or that it is a stock photo and you've received permission to use it. If not, you must seek permission for the use of any piece of art that you don't own. Consider whether the image is clear, unblemished and true in colour, especially if it is a photograph of a person. A bad photograph or illustration can easily detract from the title or even the contents of the book. Your cover will capture attention all right, but not the kind you want.

Review the guidelines for choice of art and photos for the text on page 63; the same rules will apply for the cover.

If you plan to use an archival family photo in your family history, reserve it for the inside of the book. Unless it is a person of such prominence as to be immediately recognizable by all the members of your family, it will receive better treatment inside the book where a caption can explain all the reader needs to know about the scene, people or person depicted.

As discussed earlier, do not use a "negative" photo, that is, an unpleasant photo of a nasty thing, person or place. Virtually nothing can detract more from a book.

RULE FOUR: Match Your Cover to the Subject

Just as crayon cover art doesn't suit your family history, neither does a dour portrait. It seems obvious that certain books should look certain ways, yet many people apparently miss the point.

It is not clichéd—but rather, appropriate—to make your family history look dignified. You might be a big fan of the colour combination of hot pink and electric yellow, but that doesn't mean it will do for the book. That picture of your twin cousins covered in birthday cake might be cute, but does it convey the right message?

Yet some folks seem to think that rules are made to be broken. Certainly, if you've got an artistic flair (and this talent is confirmed by others) go ahead and design as you please. Be bold, be brave and be prepared that—just maybe—your readers won't share your enthusiasm.

RULE FIVE: See Rule One

It happens to the most experienced book designers: They just can't get it right. It happens to publishers too: Their book designers just can't get it right. You'll know when this happens to you, because you won't be happy with the look of the book.

There's only one course of action. Put aside the concept, the colours, the treatment, and start over. Just as you have been wise enough to throw away a sentence in your text that didn't work, you must feel that way about the cover design. A bad

---

AN EASY SOLUTION

You can create a lovely cover by:

1. Making a box shape on paper, either on your computer or by hand. Its shape should conform to the shape of the book; in other words, a rectangular book would have a rectangular box.
2. Place your title inside the box, with type styled as you wish.
3. Put a nice border on the box.
4. Develop an overall treatment, either a solid colour or a pattern, for the area outside the text box.
5. Put the box and the background together.

You can start by creating the box shape or start with the overall background: the background could be as simple as a piece of beautiful handmade paper—which you then "tip" (see page 51) your type box onto—or something more complex.

cover usually can't be revived, and by throwing it out you'll save yourself the anguish of trying *ad nauseam* slight adjustments that for some reason still don't salvage the work.

Instead, clear your brain, try some more research in your local bookstore and then let the same inspiration that drove you to put all those words on paper guide you toward making a cover you love.

THE SPINE

Spines must be functional first and decorative second. Be sure you've got the necessary information in the customary order: title, author, publisher. Make certain that you design the type to fit the space available. Remember, some books, such as those that are saddlestitched (stapled through the spine), handsewn or Cerlox bound with plastic rings, have no spine.

Then, if you have the space and the creative knack, you can include a photo or illustration. A photo on the spine can be really eye-catching. Something like this can make your book stand out on the shelf.

THE BACK COVER

While it's very important to engage the reader by the look of the front cover, the back cover must take that interest to the next level. The back cover is a selling proposition, short and sweet. You've got about 100 words to convince readers that this is a book they want to read. The back cover can transform a browser into a buyer.

There are two separate, though related, issues to deal with in putting together the back cover—its overall design and its copy.

BACK COVER DESIGN

Many of the rules about front-cover design also apply to the back of the book: Keep the treatment simple, appropriate to the contents and easy to read. It's a good idea to keep your type on the large side (say, 14/16 pts). Make sure that the background is light in colour, and the type is dark, so there will be enough contrast between the two to make the words easy to read. If the copy you've written doesn't fit in the space available, edit or rewrite your copy. But don't reduce the type size to squeeze it all in.

Make sure there's lots of space around the words on the back cover—avoid crowding too much on. And finally, if you've styled your type and it doesn't look right, that usually means it's not right. Go to your bookshelf for inspiration and try again!

THE ISBN AND BAR CODE

The ISBN for the book is repeated on the back cover to simplify the reordering process by bookstores.

The bar code is printed on the back for the booksellers to track the book through their ordering/inventory system. It is unlikely as a home publisher that you will acquire a bar code; the ISBN and your press name is sufficient. You can find book-industry bar code software on the Internet.

OUR OWN COVER

This book began with a cover design much more complex than what you see now. Our designer, Dave Murphy at ArtPlus, thought that it would be appropriate to include an illustration or photo of a book. Unfortunately, we just couldn't find an illustration that felt right. After several tries, the all-type treatment suggested by our senior editor at the publishing house seemed the best route.

TEMPLATES

The templates in the appendix will give you some ideas for structuring your front cover.

CHAPTER 7

GETTING
READY TO
PRINT

Now that you have the manuscript written, the book designed and pages made up to your satisfaction, either on your own printer, typewriter or designer's system, the fun part begins. The part called book production, in which the pages become a printed book. The part that thousands of writers hope to achieve and so very few actually do.

And yet, book production is not an intimidating task; you'll find many people willing to give you a hand—from the person at the copy shop who'll be photocopying your colour covers (if you go that route) to your printer's sales rep (if you go with one). But if you know the basics that follow in these chapters, you'll be in a much better position to assess the value of that help and make the appropriate decisions.

THE IMPORTANCE OF PLANNING

There are two factors to take into consideration as you begin to plan the production of your book: how many copies of the finished book you need to suit your purpose, which is called the print run, and how many pages will be in your book. These factors will determine which method of reproduction and binding is right for you.

The Print Run

How many books do you want? You will need to know this to accurately plan print production. Make a list of who you will give the book to, because even if you intend to sell the book, there will still be a number of family members and friends, for instance, to whom you will undoubtedly want to give a copy.

Maybe you plan to only give your book away. Even so, that list will help you make sure you haven't forgotten someone, and it will help to focus your thoughts about where the copies are going once the book is actually completed.

If your plans include selling the book, be modest in your assessment of how many copies you need to start with. There are two good reasons for this: firstly, you can always print more books if you run out, and secondly, you won't tie up a chunk of cash unnecessarily in the expense of printing (and in storage later).

The Number of Pages

Book printers print in "forms." At one time, forms were a frame in which metal type was fastened to allow printing or plate making. Now, such frames aren't used, but the word "forms" persists. Books are comprised of sections, called forms, that consist of eight pages, or a multiple of eight. Thus you should plan your book to meet this requirement.

While it is true that, if you're printing the pages yourself on a computer printer or having them photocopied, you are not restricted to forms, if you do change your method of production to offset printing, it is much easier to have the book organized this way from the beginning than to go back and try and force it into forms. Who is not to say that your first printing won't be such a success that you won't be going back to increase your print run? Planning in forms can just make book production easier in the long run.

THE NEAREST EIGHT

You can make your book either come up or go down to the nearest eight by using a few tricks in the publishing trade:

- Add a half-title page. This is the very first page in the book. Instead of being a proper title page, it shows only the title of the book. It's followed by a blank on its reverse, adding two pages to your total.
- Add a dedication page. There's usually someone in a writer's life who merits such a reward. Again, it is usually followed by a blank, making it good for two pages.
- Add a foreword or introduction (a definition of each can be found in *The Chicago Manual of Style*). These usually add at least two pages.
- Start each new chapter on a right-hand page. This can add many pages, depending on your chapter count.
- Start the index on a right-hand page and enlarge the type size used for the index. This can bring the pages up by three or more.
- As a last resort, add blanks at the end. Unbelievable as it may seem, it is often more economical to include these unprinted pages than it is to end the book in what (to a printer) is an odd number of pages.

Alternatively, if you have included any of the first three elements in your book, you can remove them to bring down the page count to that magic number of the eight multiple.

Many books are "folio'd," that is, their pages are numbered so as to make it appear that this rule of eight is not in effect. However, if you combine the numbered text pages with the sometimes unnumbered (or sometimes numbered in roman numerals) preliminary pages, you will virtually always arrive at a multiple of eight.

Though the number of pages is driven by the content, remember two things while developing your book, because they affect the number of pages:

1. Paper is expensive. If there's ever doubt as to the contribution of an element of the book and, just maybe, that element doesn't really add to the overall strength of the work, leave it out. It will not only save you the additional expense of the extra paper and ink for printing, it will probably make the book stronger editorially too.

2. Despite number 1, never compromise the important elements of design to fit more words onto each page. Yes, you can reduce the number of pages this way, but cramming too much type on the page is a mistake you don't want to make.

HOW TO PUT QUANTITY AND SIZE TOGETHER

The following chart brings together both size of the print run with the number of pages to help you decide whether your book is suitable for reproduction by hand, digitally or by offset printing.

This chart is only a guideline. While it is quite possible to saddlestitch (meaning stapled two or three times through the centre fold of the book), 750 copies of the eight-page geneal-

No. of Copies	No. of Pages				
	32	64	96	128–356	356+
1–9					
10–24					
25–99					
100–499					
500 +					

Handmade   Digital Reproduction   Offset Printing

ogy book you prepared, the overriding assumption is that you are simply going to choose a more efficient method of putting these pages together. This chart is based on that notion.

Handmade

Handmade doesn't necessarily mean tacky. There are many beautiful works of book art that have been made by their authors in just such small quantities. In the following chapter we'll describe how you can easily reproduce the pages of your book, add a cover and bind both together for posterity.

Digital

Digital reproduction includes everything from good old photo-copying to high-tech digital printing.

In this "between" zone you've got plenty of room for creativity, because digital printing offers lots of flexibility. In Chapter 9 we will describe the methods of digital reproduction.

Offset

Ah, every author's dream: to be going to press. Offset printing, with its corresponding binding options, is the traditional book-manufacturing route. You'll find how to navigate this procedure in Chapter 10.

There are other options, particularly for binding, that aren't covered here. You could decide, for instance, to three-hole punch your book pages and insert them in binders. Binders are a good utilitarian way of holding a lot of pages together, but using a binder produces, well... a binder, not what is customarily considered to be "a book." So, our attention in the following pages will be focused on producing a book—in its more-or-less usual interpretation—of your own.

COST VS. LOST OPPORTUNITY

The cost of producing a book is not only in continual flux because of ups and downs in the paper market, but also—as you're about to appreciate in the following pages—because there are so many variables.

It is only to be expected that whatever you do yourself is the cheapest; after all, you're the labour! Therefore, by extrapolation, the handmade method is the least expensive. The cost for digital printing is higher and the cost for a manufactured book the highest.

Yet perhaps it's not fair to book printers to single them out as the most expensive route for production. Offset may cost the most, but the finished product has production values that other forms usually can't match. When you're thinking about which method of production is the best given your ultimate plans for your book, it may be worthwhile to factor in professional appearance versus the dollars involved. In all likelihood, you will want your book to look good and be durable, whether the market is friends, family or the local bookshop. It doesn't matter if you're giving the book away or selling it, if it doesn't measure up, then you haven't saved money at all.

CHAPTER 8

MADE BY
HAND

In the previous chapter we determined that making your book by hand was the best option if your book has 64 pages or less, and if you wanted less than 100 copies for distribution.

Handmade books are an art form that has been on the wane since Mr. Gutenberg printed his first volume in the 15th century. You should take real pride in the task before you, because the results can be beautiful, even if you feel you are artistically challenged!

The process of making a book by hand begins with deciding how to put the words on the page. Then you must determine how to reproduce the pages in the book, how to produce an attractive cover and finally how to bind the pages and cover together.

REPRODUCTION MUST START WITH AN ORIGINAL

Before you can have multiple copies of a book, you must start with one good version which we will call the original. It is from the original that the copies are made. When you are producing a hand-made book, there are three ways to go about creating the original:

- handwriting
- a typewriter
- a computer linked to a laser printer

Handwriting

Before printing was invented, every single book was written by hand. Scribes prided themselves on the beauty of their hand-writing, and by combining words with decorative elements, called illumination, they created magnificent books that were enjoyed by a select few.

Although extremely rare, handwriting the pages in your book is still an option, if the handwriting is up to the task.

Handwritten pages could add a personal touch to your family history. The key to a successful handwritten book is not to have too many words on each page. Quite often one sees recipe books compiled as fundraisers in which all the

---

CALLIGRAPHY

The art of beautiful handwriting has made a real resurgence over the past few years. Many craft shops, stationers and even toy shops stock the tools of the trade for those who want to try their hand at this art form.

Calligraphy could be wonderful on book pages, whether created by you or by someone you hire. It would be especially appropriate to use when decorative type is called for: the title of the book, the chapter names or even the names of treasured family recipes.

ingredients and cooking instructions have been handwritten. The writing compels your attention, so that you don't see how good the recipes might be. This points to the biggest problem with handwriting the text: the handwriting can detract—or distract—from the content.

If you are going to handwrite your text you will want to:

1. Make sure your handwriting is absolutely legible.
2. Try to keep the writing consistent throughout all the pages: use the same pen, write on the same surface and try to form your letters in a similar style throughout.
3. Don't print everything in capital letters: in the e-mail world this is called shouting—and for good reason—because it is just too heavy-handed.
4. Be neat. Rule your pages very lightly, using a non-reproducing blue pencil or hard lead pencil to keep your writing on an even keel. If you make a mistake, it's better to do the page over than erase. This is for posterity, remember!
5. Keep all your margins the same on every page. Medieval monks used to plan their pages before committing ink to parchment by carefully calculating how the words would fit on the page. You should do the same. Then you won't be left with one last page and only two words to fill it!

Plan to handwrite one perfect copy and then reproduce it following the advice on the next page. Don't try to write multiple copies: there are, simply, better ways of producing copies than individually handwriting them.

Typewriting

Despite what some advocates of computer technology would have us think, there are still many people who only have access to a typewriter. A typewriter can be a quite acceptable way of producing pages, especially if it is electric.

Typewritten pages are acceptable for a family history. If you are going to typewrite your text:

1. Put in a new ribbon and keep putting in new ribbons if the book is a longish one to keep the type consistently black throughout the book.
2. Buy a new jar of liquid corrector, or a new erasing ribbon to fix mistakes neatly.
3. Don't type all in capital letters.
4. Use a good dictionary to hyphenate words correctly.
5. Leave lots of space between the rows of type. A page filled from top to bottom margin with row upon row of typewritten words does not invite reading. Make good use of white space. (See Chapter 5.)

Duplicating Handwritten or Typewritten Originals

Once you have your handwritten or typewritten original completed, take it to your local copy shop for duplication. You will have to choose between one- or two-sided copying. One-sided will always look like a collection of loose pages; two-sided more closely approximates printing. If you choose the latter, make certain that the two pages "back up" properly—that is, that their margins match and the type from one page overlays the type on the other when viewed together. Imagine holding the page up to the light: you will want the type to cover the same area on each side of the page.

The real bonus to photocopying as a method of duplication is that, unlike the case with offset printing, you are not bound by forms. Therefore your book does not have to be in the multiple of eight, because it is not being produced on a press.

Computer/Laser Printer

Well, there's just no way around this: The computer/laser printer combination is the best way to produce an original for every kind of book. Not only do you have an enormous array of typefaces and type sizes available, but mistakes can be fixed without a trace.

Plus, this is the one case when you can actually produce more than a single copy of the pages, and still keep sane. If you're producing, say, a half-dozen copies of an eight-page family tree, just print off all the copies of the pages you need and save the expense of going elsewhere.

If you are printing the pages of a book that will be saddle-stitched (again, this means stapled two or three times through the centre fold of the book)—whether you are printing the pages off your computer or you are taking them to a photocopy shop that will reproduce the pages—you will need to set your pages up in "printer's spreads." This is because you are not producing single pages of the book but double pages. Double pages are called spreads.

You can very easily calculate these spreads for yourself. Simply fold together pieces of paper that will result in the correct number of pages in your book and write the page number on each page. Remember that each sheet of paper yields four book pages. When you take them apart you will find that the paper looks like the illustration on the following page (for a 16-page book):

1st sheet: side 1		reverse		2nd sheet: side 1		reverse	
page no.	page no.	page no.	page no.	page no.	page no.	page no.	page no.
16	1	2	15	14	3	4	13

3rd sheet: side 1		reverse		4th sheet: side 1		reverse	
page no.	page no.	page no.	page no.	page no.	page no.	page no.	page no.
12	5	6	11	10	7	8	9

Then stack the sheets with page 1 on top, followed by 3, 5 and 7, and your book will be perfectly paged.

To achieve printer's spreads on your laser printer you will be printing on your page horizontally (usually called landscape orientation) to create two book pages side by side on each piece of paper. By using paper that is 8-1/2 x 14" you will be able to produce a book with a finished size of about 6-1/2 x 8-1/2" (not 7 x 8-1/2") because you need some extra space to trim the pages. More on this later. You may need to buy a paper tray for your printer that can handle the longer length, but it's worth the expense to save the aggravation—and paper waste—of feeding individual sheets through on a shorter tray.

If you are not saddlestitching the book, you will be producing single pages that will be sewn, wiro- or Cerlox bound. To do this, simply print out a single page for every page in the book, or multiple copies if the number of books you're producing is few. Cerlox or wiro-binding is usually done at a photocopy shop. If you're handsewing, see pages 105–106.

When printing from a laser printer, make sure to use proper laser paper, not photocopy paper or bond paper. Laser paper really makes a big difference to the print quality.

A final word: If you do not have access to a laser printer, set up your "print file" on a CD and take it to a service bureau such as a photocopy shop, where it can be output to a laser printer. When you've come this far, don't sell yourself short by using a lower-quality printer.

COVER UPS

Now that you've got the inside pages finished, you will need to select a cover material (this heavy paper is known as cover stock) that is attractive, and appropriate for the finished product. You also need to choose one that is suitable for the binding method you have in mind.

Creating the Handmade Book Cover

There are three ways you can easily create a cover for your book.

1. The Do-It-Yourself Method: Draw your own cover art or design the cover on your computer and print it out. If you're producing more than one copy, you'll have to duplicate the original. Photocopying, whether in colour or black and white, is probably your best bet. Affix the cover art to your cover stock.
2. Use preprinted materials to give an overall pattern for the cover. Affix this material to stock that is suitable for use as a cover.
3. Die-cut either plain or preprinted paper (see pages 102–103 about die-cutting) to reveal an illustration or the title on the first page of the book.

Do-It-Yourself

Following all the advice in this book you have created front-cover art that makes you happy. Whether you have done this by hand or machine makes no difference as long as it works for you.

THE LOOK OF CANVAS, ON PAPER

If you are printing your covers off your computer, and your design includes a colour photograph or illustration, you might want to look into a product by Xerox called Canvas Paper. This paper has a texture like the canvas used in oil painting. Used properly, the effects of printing on such paper can be quite beautiful.

Duplicate the number of copies of the art that you need for the number of copies you are producing, and make yourself a couple of spares in case you need to experiment or there's an accident during the binding process. You can make these copies by printing in colour from your computer, by taking your file on disk to a service bureau where they can print it in colour for you or by colour photocopying.

The paper you use for the cover for your book can be either the same weight as the text paper, or, for greater durability and a more professional appearance, a heavier weight paper. Heavier stock also gives the option of die-cutting, which is not really possible with text-weight paper.

A very accessible choice for a heavier stock is any card-type stock, such as Bristol board. Cut the board to the size you need. Remember, in a saddlestitched book this board is going to wrap around the entire book. You will want to apply your front cover art to the part of the board that will become the front cover, using either spray adhesive or rubber cement. If you have prepared back cover art, it needs to go on too. Be careful that you apply the "art" so that it is square and properly aligned. Then, by using a wonderful product called GEO Multi Fix Adhesive Film you can add a smooth shiny finish to the cover, giving it the look of lamination. Multi Fix is available in well-equipped office supply stores and is very inexpensive. Although Multi Fix claims to be removable, it does tend to also remove part of the top layer of the paper to which it has been adhered when you lift it. Therefore, it's a good idea to experiment with some first, so when you lay it down you can just leave it there.

VIEW OF THE OUTSIDE COVER OF A
SADDLESTITCHED BOOK SHOWING COPY LAYOUT

Back Cover   Front Cover

If you're making a saddlestitched book, you'll then have to prepare the "cover" for folding at its centre line. Bristol board can be ugly when folded unless you score it first. To score the board, first draw a line where you want the board to fold. Then, using a straight edge and a blunt, but pointed, instrument such as a letter opener or unopened pair of scissors, run the instrument lightly along the straight edge, making a faint crease in the board. This is called scoring. Be careful not to actually cut the board. You might have to score the line several times until the board will fold easily and neatly. However, don't fold it closed yet. Wait until you've place your pages inside, and have inserted the staples through the spine. Then, fold the book closed.

If you are handsewing or Cerlox binding the book, you will be dealing with two sheets of "cover" paper instead of the wrap-around sheet you use in saddlestitching. Bristol board with your art and Multi Fix on top is still a good route to go for the front cover. Although you could dispense with the back cover, it's a nice finishing touch to put a heavy-weight stock on the back that gives the work a more solid feel.

Preprinted Materials

Preprinted materials include an enormous variety of possibilities: wallpaper, handmade paper, fabric, Con-Tact®, gift wrap— you name it. Such paper generally becomes the design of the cover, as it would look odd to add type on over such overall patterns. However, type can go in a type box and then be pasted over the pattern of your material.

However, frequently such materials are so beautiful that they make a powerful statement on their own. This is your personal decision.

To use such materials, you will probably have to laminate them to a sturdier stock. Experiment with rubber cement, starch paste and spray adhesive to see which works successfully. Once applied to the standard cover stock, the preprinted material cover is treated like any other.

Die-cutting

In true die-cutting, a metal die stamps its way through the material being die cut. This creates a hole in the shape of the die. You're obviously not going to create a metal die, but with an X-acto blade, steady hand and your imagination you can create wonderful die-cut designs and patterns.

In die-cutting you are using both the cover and the first book page to create your design art. The art will be a combination of the shape of the hole being cut in the cover and the colour or illustration on the first book page which appears through the hole.

Die-cutting, in effect, is using a negative image (a hole) in a very positive way. The hole can become the design (if the die-cutting is done in the shape of the sun and stars, for instance), or the hole can reveal the design (if the hole shows an illustration on the page). You can combine die-cutting with the use of preprinted materials for a number of interesting effects.

To die-cut successfully, you really need a paper with some body, so plan to use Bristol board with Multi Fix on top. Plan your design carefully. If the die-cut comes too close to the spine or outside edges of the book, it can weaken the strength of the cover.

Die-cutting offers tremendously exciting possibilities, but it is a true one-off procedure. Every cover you do this way will be an original, so you might want to use this technique only when a very few number of copies are being produced.

A BINDING SITUATION

Ah, yet more choices to make! You're probably getting a good sense of why publishing is such a creative endeavour.

If we return to the section of our original matrix (page 91) that indicated we were going to make a book by hand because of the number of copies and number of pages in the book, we

No. of Copies	No. of Pages					
	8	16	32	64		Saddlestitching
1–9						
10–24						Handsewing
25–99						Fasteners or Cerlox

can now work within those parameters to arrive at a logical way of binding the pages and cover together.

Saddlestitching is a good durable way of holding the pages and cover together. It is inexpensive, and looks professional. After all, publishers produce saddlestitched books all the time, particularly for the children's market.

In saddlestitching, two or three staples are forced through the centre fold of the book from the cover into the middle of the book. This way, the rough edges of the staples are buried on the inside of the book.

You will have had to plan saddlestitching your book from the start of the production process to ensure that you have prepared your text in printer's spreads (see pages 97–98) and your cover as a wraparound. With that done, it is a simple matter to attach your pages to the cover on the top and bottom edges with paper clamps, slide the stapler in to where it is properly positioned to staple through the centre of the book and apply two or three staples at regular intervals. (If the span of the stapler is too short to reach the centre of the book, you'll have to find a bigger one. You can buy a stapler that's big enough or have your stapling done at a copy shop.)

When you fold your book in half, the pages in the middle of the book are going to protrude. This is called shingling. Printers have all kinds of fancy ways of dealing with this, but for the home publisher it is best to simply allow yourself a good wide margin on all the pages in the book and, using a really good paper cutter, trim that vertical edge so that all the pages line up evenly.

Your saddlestitched book is now complete!

Handsewing

Handsewing is a way of attaching loose sheets with their covers. The best technique for handsewing is called the Japanese binding stitch. But before you get out your needle, you will have to produce five absolutely aligned holes in each complete book you plan to sew. With some patience this can be achieved. First, make a master sheet, with the holes in place. Using the master, and lining up the pages carefully every time, mark the holes on your pages. Then, if you want a very fine binding, use an awl to create the actual holes in the pages. You can make bigger holes by using a single-hole paper punch.

Whatever size hole you end up with, you will want to match the sewing thread accordingly. Embroidery thread would be lovely with small holes, but plastic lacing, also called "gimp," or even a shoelace would be more suitable for large holes. It would be very appropriate to use butcher string to handsew a history of a family of ranchers! One word of caution: The thread should not have much give to it, or with any degree of use the binding will become very sloppy.

The illustration below gives all you need to know to master the binding stitch. Start at the back and you will end at the back;

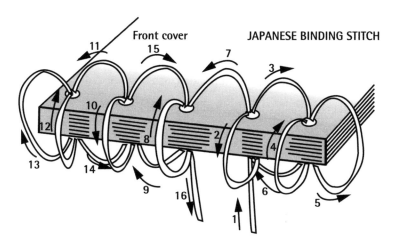

JAPANESE BINDING STITCH

knot the ends neatly and securely. Just make sure you use a long enough piece of thread, rope or lacing to begin with: All this back and forth sewing eats up the thread very quickly.

Cerlox or Fasteners

Virtually any copy shop can provide Cerlox binding. It's cheap, and it does allow the pages in the book to lie flat. For this reason, it's quite popular for cookbooks and other instructional guides. However, it just isn't very good-looking and it can fall apart quite quickly if one or two rings are inadvertently pulled out.

Instead of Cerlox binding, have your book and cover three-hole punched at your local copy shop, or do it yourself. Inserting brass fasteners through the holes makes a very simple, long-lasting but handsome way of holding the book together.

Another alternative is to use grommets. Again, you will need to have your pages pre-punched with holes. Using a grommet tool, insert the grommets into the holes and lock them in place. Grommets are available in a number of colours, any of which are very attractive. You will need to monitor the thickness of your book closely to ensure that the grommets will fit—and hold.

Regardless of what binding option you choose, by taking the time to plan your production carefully—from the design of the pages and cover through their duplication—you will be able to produce a professional-looking handmade book that may well become a family heirloom.

CHAPTER 9

THE TECHNOLOGICAL PRINTING SOLUTION

It may lack the poetry of making a book by hand, and the ease of giving a CD to a printer with a purchase order, but technology in the form of digital printing gives you an efficient and professional way of producing a book.

FINDING A DIGITAL PRINTER

There are photocopy shops around that call themselves digital printers, when in fact they photocopy the pages of your book in just the same way that you would if you had a photocopy machine at your disposal. Then there are digital printers who offer very high-end solutions to digital printing. You will want to make sure you match your needs to what is available.

You can find digital printers in the *Yellow Pages*. You should call a few to discuss your project and get a cost quotation.

If your book is being reproduced in black only, the photocopy shop is the answer. On the other hand, if you have included colour pages of art, photos or illustrations, you should look to the more sophisticated digital printer.

THE PHOTOCOPY SHOP

Photocopy equipment can print on paper that is either 8-1/2 x 11", 8-1/2 x 14" or 11 x 17". The large size allows you to make up your pages in a printer's spread format, as shown on page 98, if two facing pages can be accommodated on one sheet of paper. In this way, you will enjoy the cost savings of "printing" two pages with one click.

Clicks are how photocopy shops price their work: every copy is a click. Using good old white bond paper, about the lowest per click cost is $0.035, so if your book has 100 pages and you need 100 copies, the photocopying cost will be $175 (with two pages per click). If you upgrade the kind of paper you use, that cost will be additional, as will the cost of covers and binding.

BOTH SIDES NOW

If you deliver single pages to the photocopy shop for duplicating, make sure the paper is photocopied double-sided for a more appropriate book-type appearance. It's also a good idea to see how your pages "back up"—that is, the type should cover the same area on the page front and back. If this isn't happening correctly, you may need to have the setup adjusted in the copying or—horrors!—go back to your page setup to make the necessary changes.

Covers can be colour copied on a coated (shiny) or uncoated (not shiny) card stock. Binding options include Cerlox, wiro-binding or coil binding, thermal binding and, occasionally, perfectbinding. Thermal binding uses a tape that is affixed along the spine of the book to hold the pages together. The maximum number of pages that can be bound with thermal binding is about 125.

Among the many advantages of the photocopy route is the speed with which your book can be produced and your ability to make as few copies of the book as you need. You can have just one book copied and bound, and, if the shop isn't busy, that book could be ready in a day. When you need another, back you go. Even though the cost is higher on a per-copy basis to copy one set of pages instead of 100, you won't be out of pocket in the meantime.

The photocopy route might be especially fitting if your book is a "work in progress." Let's say you want to get as much of that family history as you have written to date duplicated and distributed in order to seek contributions from far-away family members. Then it's a great idea to take as much of your book as you have ready and prepare it in a professional, well-designed manner to encourage relatives to read it. Photocopy these pages, Cerlox bind them and send them out. When the comments, new stories and queries come back and your manuscript is finally complete, you may decide that another method of duplication best suits your long-term purpose.

PRINT ON DEMAND

True digital printing is very similar to offset printing because, unlike photocopying, the ink used for printing is a liquid and not a powder. However, unlike offset printing, a laser puts a new image on the plate with every revolution of the press. This makes every page an original.

Print on demand offers many more options than photo-copying. Paper size can be up to 12" x 18", and a wide variety of different types of paper are available. Stocks can include those that are coated; they are the ideal choice for the reproduction of colour.

And this is where print on demand shines. This technology prints colour beautifully. Meanwhile, your print run can be only one copy; there's no penalty for a small print run. What's more, you are spared one of the largest expenses in producing a colour book: the film from which the plates are made. Print on demand uses digital images instead of film.

There are a number of requirements to meet in the correct preparation of the file for print on demand. It's best for you to go over this in detail with a sales representative at the printer to ensure that your application can be supported (i.e., that the printer is able to work with the program you are using) and that you are preparing your file to the printer's specifications.

This may be the ideal solution for you if you want to pro-duce a small run of a full-colour book.

Print on demand services will also print your cover and bind your book as you choose. You will achieve a much better result than photocopying, and many services offer templates that make designing your cover easy.

BINDING

How you will bind your digitally reproduced book—whether photocopied or digitally printed—will depend entirely on the number of pages in your book, whether it is formatted for saddlestitching and how many copies of the book you have produced.

Binding a few copies with few pages in each is addressed in Chapter 8 under the discussion of making books by hand. Binding more copies of many pages is addressed in Chapter 10 about offset printing.

OFFSET
PRINTING:
GOING TO PRESS

It seems pretty reasonable to assume that, if you want hundreds of copies or more of your book, you're going to do more than give it to your family. This quantity demands the highest degree of professionalism in your approach to printing and binding. After all, your book needs to look credible in order to attain the level of acceptance you're seeking. You need a professional book printer.

HOW TO FIND A PRINTER

As with most things in life, a recommendation from another customer is the best way of finding a company that you'll feel confident working with. But if you're on your own in this department, and most home-publishing authors are, there are several sources to which you can turn.

The Book Trade in Canada is a reference book that your library should have; it includes a section on Printers, Binders & Related Services. This section lists many of the big players, but even if only a large printer is located in your area, that company could refer you to a small press for your printing.

Scott's Directories is another library reference that can help. All types of business activities are categorized by SIC code number. Book printers are found under the SIC code 2732. Scott's will give the company contact information you'll need for names, phone and fax numbers and address.

Your local *Yellow Pages* can help you find printers, though the ads may not specify which firms are *book* printers. This will be the most difficult list to wade through; however, with any luck, you'll get some advice on finding a book company by speaking with a sales rep at any firm listed.

QUESTIONS TO ASK A PRINTER

Once you're clear that the quantity of books you want requires a book printer, you should start calling printers to obtain cost quotations.

If you've had to pick some printing companies at random from your *Yellow Pages*, you need to establish some groundwork for the type of printing they do. Then you'll be ready to proceed with the specifics of whether your needs and their services match.

Ask:

May I speak to someone in the sales department?

This is the place to start your discussion about your book. Printers' sales reps are very knowledgeable about book production. Usually book printers are enormously helpful, especially when you are just learning about book manufacturing. Tell the person you speak to that you are home publishing; it will help to focus the conversation on your needs versus those of a publishing company.

Do you manufacture books?

Manufacturing a book means the capability to carry out the entire process of producing a book. In theory, all printers could print the pages of a book, but if they have no way of binding the pages, because they usually print flyers, brochures or other loose-leaf materials, then they are not book manufacturers. It is best to avoid printing pages in one place, and binding the pages in another. Keep looking until you find a book manufacturer: It will make your job easier, and a lot more fun, if there are people to work with who understand books and who will share the benefit of their experience with you.

Can you print the quantity of books I need?

This point should come out almost immediately in your discussion with the sales rep. Some printers specialize in large print runs; others can do very modest amounts. Their willingness to print a small run may also be directly related to the time of year you plan to print. From July through early December, book printers are frantically filling publishers' orders. Their ability or willingness to accommodate you during this period may be limited, because the presses are running full out on large (read: profitable) runs. Come January or February, it may be a different story. Presses are idle and manufacturers are looking for work. At such a time, they may well be prepared to do a small printing.

THE BEST TIME?

Printing in the first quarter of the year may have its advantages in both the cost of the printing and the manufacturers' willingness to take on your job. If you plan to sell your book, remember that fall is the peak season for book sales and delivery to fill these sales usually occurs in August or September. If you plan to give away your book at Christmas, there may be a ten-month lapse between printing and your need for finished books. In other words, you've got a storage problem. Weigh the cost and inconvenience of storage against the savings in printing cost to see if you really are better off to print sooner instead of later.

How long will it take to deliver the finished book?

To answer this, the printer will need details on what type of book you plan to manufacture. These are called the "specifications" and are covered below in detail. However, you should generally calculate between four weeks to three months for finished books. Again, there are many variables affecting this process, such as the format in which you are delivering materials to the printer (for instance, whether you are supplying scanned photos on a CD, or originals that the printer will need to either scan or otherwise shoot); the complexity of the printing (one colour or four?); anything special you want in your book, such as those handmade marbleized endpapers that must be custom ordered from Italy, and the time of year. However, if time is an issue to you because you want the book for a certain date, tell the printer this when you are discussing the job. If time has become short, your choices in finding a printer—and how much you will have to pay—may be affected.

What are your payment terms?

Be prepared to pay for your order when you confirm the job with the printer, whether by a letter or a purchase order. Many printers have lost significant amounts of money when established publishers go out of business, so they will rarely risk investing their time and materials for payment at the end of the process when it is an individual, or even a small company, ordering the work.

What about your risk? Is there a chance that the book won't meet your expectations and you'll have paid for a product you're not satisfied with? The answer when working with an experienced book manufacturer is "no." If you have correctly specified what you want and when you want it, there should be no surprises. If, on the other hand, your printer is dear old Uncle Bob's almost-best friend who runs a small press in his basement, you must guard yourself against the worst. Insist on viewing work samples before starting, and then negotiate payment terms. Terms are often based on paying some money up front, some on completion of printing and some on completion of binding. Your approvals along the way will ensure that you know what you're getting.

A BOOK PRINTER OR A BOOK MANUFACTURER?

The word "printer" is used synonymously with "manufacturer." Manufacturer is actually the correct term, because there is much more to the process of making a book than printing it, but, like so much in the publishing business that hinges on the traditional, "printer" is preferred.

READY TO QUOTE

There are many, many variables in developing an accurate cost quotation for the manufacture of a book. Unless you're one of the lucky few to whom cost is no object, you will want to plan out your specifications carefully, then circulate them to at least three manufacturers for comparison. In publishing houses, it isn't necessarily the cheapest quote which gets the job; it will often be the company that has earned the work through the quality of service it offers. This same factor might affect your decision, too.

Here are the headings you should have on your Request for Quotation:

Title: _____

Quantity: _____

Size of the finished book (trim size): _____

Number of pages: _____

Preparation: Text, cover and/or jacket: _____

Paper: Text: _____

If softcover: Paper: Cover: _____

If hardcover: Materials: Case _____

           Paper: Jacket _____

           Paper: Endpapers _____

Printing: Text: _____

If softcover: Printing: Cover: _____

If hardcover: Printing: Case: _____

           Printing: Jacket: _____

           Printing: Endpapers: _____

Binding: _____

Finished book date: _____

Shipping: _____

Here's how to complete the information under each heading:

Title

This is simply a way of keeping track of what is being quoted at the manufacturer's. If you haven't decided on a title, just use your name.

Quantity

Now this is essential information to know up front, and while you can change your mind about how many copies of the book you want, it really is discourteous to go back to the printer over and over again with a different quantity each time.

Think quantity through carefully. True, you may not have any idea how much your book will cost, but it will not be cheap, no matter how you produce it. Paper is an expensive commodity. So, who is your market? How realistic are your goals? For some guidance on this subject, refer to the final chapter in this book. Meanwhile, be conservative. If you start small, and your book is a runaway success, you can always have the thrill of going back to press for more copies. This is a great feeling compared to looking at hundreds of "extra" books in permanent storage in your basement.

Also remember that printing is subject to overages and underages. Overages are caused because the press simply can't be stopped at exactly the number of copies you want, and underages are caused for the same reason in addition to some books being destroyed during binding. Printers may specify 10% either way on your quantity to provide this allowance. At the end of the day, you're going to pay for overages, so be prepared for the additional expense.

Size

Trim size is how printers describe the size of the finished book. You have already determined the trim size that is appropriate to the type of book you are producing, but it still makes sense to ask your printer about whether the trim size you've selected is a good fit for their presses. If it isn't, you'll probably see that fact reflected in the cost quotation, and it can explain why one printer's quote will be substantially higher than another's. You just may need to keep shopping for the printer that's right for you.

Number of pages

As discussed in Chapter 7, books are planned to be printed in forms comprised of eight pages. Specify your number of pages rounded up or down to the nearest multiple of eight.

Preparation – Text, Cover and/or Jacket

If you are producing a four-colour text, cover or jacket (see page 124), it's likely that you'll need to have the film for those elements produced at a company that specializes in producing film for printing. This kind of company is called a film house, and one can be located through a recommendation from the printer or your *Yellow Pages*. Coordinate your efforts between the film house and printer to ensure that you are delivering film to the printer's specification.

If your text or cover isn't in four colours, you'll have to deliver the text and cover to the printer in the format they need to produce plates. As discussed in Chapter 5, some printers might ask for camera-ready art (a somewhat antiquated expectation but still a possibility). The better the camera-ready art you supply, the better the printing will be. That is why printers like a good-quality original from which they will make film. This film is then used to make the printing plates. However, camera-ready art can be even a handwritten or typewritten manuscript, with an envelope of photographs the printer must shoot separately and combine with the text. In printer's parlance this is called "stripping," as in "The photos will have to be stripped in." This has traditionally all been part of the printing process.

Now, printers prefer to receive the text files electronically on CD or even by e-mail, with the photos or art already incorporated. You should accompany the electronic file with a paper-copy printout, and before you prepare the whole CD, make up a sample of a chapter or two to see if the CD is being prepared correctly and that all computer systems are compatible. Ask the printer how the file is to be formatted; whether the file should come from a Mac (the machine of choice in the book-design world) or PC; what program they will expect you to use for formatting (Quark XPress is common, but not the first choice for the home publisher because of its expense and level of sophistication); how the fonts should be supplied; and anything else relevant to capturing and delivering the files correctly.

Paper – Text

There seem to be about a million types of paper to use in printing a book, from the finest, whitest, heaviest virginal vellum to coarse, recycled newsprint.

Many books use a stock similar to the one used in this book: a good serviceable choice that is easy on the eyes without costing the earth. If this is a good choice for you, tell your printer you're looking for a 60 lb. cream stock. If you want something grander, you will have a wealth of choice up to 120 lb. If you have seen an existing book with paper that you admire and want for your book, it's probably best to supply your printer with a copy of the book and let the staff try to figure out what has been used or what's available that is similar.

The real issues for you may be the use of recycled paper and the acidity of the paper. If you want to use recycled paper, simply tell your printer. Paper acidity became a hot topic a few years ago when the danger of paper deterioration in modern

TYPICAL PRINTING COSTS

Some typical costs for printing home-published books at a book manufacturing plant:

Size	Page count	Printing and binding	Rough Quantity	Cost
8 x 10"	160 pages	text in black; cover in colour; softcover	1,000 copies	$7000
7 x 10"	128 pages	text in black; cover in colour; softcover	1,000 copies	$3500
8 x 8"	32 pages	text and cover printed in full colour; softcover	1,000 copies	$3500
6-1/4 x 9"	320 pages	text in black; cover in colour; softcover	1,000 copies	$4500
5-1/2 x 8-1/2"	128 pages	text in black; cover in colour; softcover	2,000 copies	$3300

Assumes same weight of paper (50 lb. offset) used for all the books and their covers (10 pt.). Note: No category has been provided for hardcover because hardcover books are very costly to produce. If you can afford such a book, you should probably pay a book designer to manage the production of the project.

books in libraries and other collections was first recognized. Paper manufacturers responded to this concern by producing acid-free book papers, and now most book paper is acid-free. If you want your book to last long after you do, specify acid-free paper to be sure that's what you're getting.

Paper – Cover

You have already determined whether you are making a cover or a jacket, but let's quickly review: a cover is the heavy printed paper encasing the pages of a softcover book, while a jacket wraps around the case of a hardcover book. You will probably choose to produce a softcover book.

Softcover books make large use of a stock called Cornwall, coated one side (C1S); the stock is virtually always 10 pt. or 12 pt., the latter being slightly heavier than the former and, correspondingly, slightly more expensive.

Covers are virtually always finished with a plastic lamination on their printed side. This coating provides a pleasant-looking sheen to the cover while also helping to protect the cover from getting dirty and torn.

Hardcover Materials – Case, Jacket and Endpapers

Case. There are so many different ways to produce a case for a book that it is impossible to describe what might or might not be a good choice. For starters, you will need to specify natural or synthetic materials. Printers have sample books showing these materials. You will need to see these samples to make your choice unless you are providing a sample of what you like and use that as your quotation reference point. On your Request for Quotation, put "See attached sample."

Jacket. Jacket paper is usually quite substantial in weight; jackets, after all, take a beating. Although book jackets look nice, they are costly to produce and easily damaged. You want your family history book to be passed down as a treasured heirloom, but if the jacket is torn after only a few years, it could detract from its aesthetic appeal. If you do choose this look, specify a 100 lb. gloss stock for the jacket and you will have a handsome jacket on your book.

Endpapers. An endpaper is the plain or patterned paper you see when you open a hardcover book. Endpapers can be white, uniformly coloured, printed or individually created by use of specialized techniques such as marbleizing. A 100 lb. offset stock will do nicely for endpapers unless you are going to create them yourself. If you are going this route, tell your printer and follow the directions for what you will need to supply to ensure the correct size and general suitability.

Printing – Text

Ever heard a book described as being printed in black and white? It's a common description for a book that is actually printed in black ink; the white, of course, is provided by the colour of the paper.

Remember then that the colour of the paper is an element for consideration. White paper will support all colour choices; a neutral-coloured paper — cream, for instance—will support the use of single dark colours, such as dark green or blue, but not four colours. A coloured stock in any strong colour (dark turquoise, neon pink, orange) is best not used.

Your choices in printing, while some would describe them as limitless, are actually a choice of:

- black
- specially coloured inks called PMS colours
- four-process colours
- a combination of four-process colours with PMS colours (rare in the commercial book world)

You must tell the printer which one of these formats you plan to use. (See page 124 for a quick explanation of colour printing processes.)

You will also need to specify whether your text pages have a "bleed"; it is always assumed by the printer that the cover or jacket will bleed, and they are quoted accordingly. A bleed is a rather unfortunate choice of words to describe whether the printing goes right to the edge of the page, or not. A full-colour photograph, for instance, that covers the entire page of the book, without any white margin showing around the outside edges, is said to bleed. If even one line across the top of the text runs off the edge, that is a bleed. Pages with a bleed can cost more to print than those without, because it may mean the printer needs to use a larger sheet of paper. If there is no bleed on your pages, you must restrict your printing within the margins set by the printer; usually these are not less than 1/4" to 3/8". It's wise to leave a greater margin than this in any case, to ensure that your print doesn't come perilously close to the edge of the page.

A QUICK PRIMER ON COLOUR

Colour on a printed page is achieved in one of two ways. To print a colour image, such as a colour photo, that photo must first be electronically scanned and broken down into its constituent parts of cyan (blue), magenta (red), yellow and black. This is called colour separation. A colour image, such as a photo, will be printed in dots of the four separate colours—cyan, magenta, yellow and black. This is called four-colour process. Various combinations of these dots can yield an infinite number of colours. Coloured type will either be printed four-colour process or by using specified PMS (Pantone Matching System) colours. PMS colours are specially premixed inks available for printers to use in an enormous array of colours, including neons and metallics. To print type in two colours is far less expensive using PMS colour than four-colour process.

If you use PMS colours in addition to four-colour process, which is possible in order to produce a book with six, eight or even the virtually unheard-of twelve-colour printing, you'll be entering the stratosphere in the expense department.

Four-colour process printing is very expensive because it requires, first of all, the scanning of the colour photographs (which can cost upwards of $50 per photo), second, the production of one sheet of film for each colour for every page in the book, with colour proofs of sufficient quality to be used during print as checks for colour, and, finally, one printing plate for each colour. Even though printers have introduced direct-to-plate four-colour technology, thereby eliminating the need for film, four-colour printing will continue to be a costly method of reproduction.

Achieving colour in a book using one or two PMS colours is much less expensive. Less film is needed and fewer plates are required. Book printers have been using direct-to-plate technology for two-colour printing for some time. This saves the expense of producing a sheet of film of each colour for every page in the book.

In order to specify what PMS colour (or colours) you want to use, you will need to consult with your printing rep to see the PMS book displaying all the colours available. Usually the colours are shown printed on a coated stock, where they appear bright and lively, and on an uncoated stock, where they appear dull in comparison. Just be aware that, if you pick a colour from the coated portion of the book and you're printing on uncoated paper, you're going to be disappointed with the result. Each ink colour in the PMS system has a code number. Record this number to specify it on your purchase order to your printer.

Printing – Cover

It is much more cost efficient to produce a book printed in black for the text and then inject a strong dose of colour on the cover. Again, you must specify four-colour process, PMS or a combination (rare) and be prepared to deliver materials to the printer accordingly.

If you are printing four-colour process, many publishers choose to deliver film for the job. In order to deliver film, you must work with a printing film supply house in order to achieve the correct output for the printer.

If your cover is making exclusive use of PMS colour, you might choose to deliver the cover on CD. Before doing this, check with the printer to see what kind of CD is acceptable and what is needed both on the CD (fonts for instance) and with the CD (an inkjet colour print, for instance). Delivering what the printer needs to do the job properly will make the whole production process easier for you and for the printer.

Hardcover Printing – Cases, Jacket and Endpapers

Cases. As previously discussed, manufacturing cases is a complicated procedure. So is their printing. Cases can be printed in four colours and laminated or foil stamped on the front and spine. You already know the demands that four-colour work places on the designer and home publisher. Stamping is fairly easily accomplished by providing the printer with the art in a format from which they can make film and, subsequently, a stamping die. You simply need to specify the colour of foil to be used.

Jackets. Jackets are virtually always printed in four-colour process, or even four-colour process plus PMS. They're pretty lavish productions, and if you're putting a jacket on your book, you might as well go all out and print four colours too. Specify four-colour process plus 1/2 mil gloss lamination to provide a nice finish and add durability.

Endpapers. Endpapers can be white or printed in one or more PMS colours or four-colour process. They can also be handmade by you, or you can purchase beautiful handmade endpapers through your printer. Assess what suits your vision and your budget.

Binding

You have a number of binding options available through your printer. The following table helps to show what binding is best for each size of book.

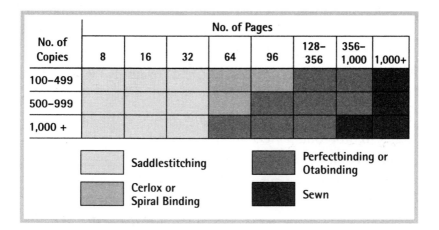

No. of Copies	No. of Pages							
	8	16	32	64	96	128–356	356–1,000	1,000+
100–499								
500–999								
1,000 +								

Saddlestitching · Perfectbinding or Otabinding · Cerlox or Spiral Binding · Sewn

Saddlestitching. As previously described, this kind of binding involves stapling through the centre of the pages. Two or three staples are customary.

This is really appropriate for—and sometimes the only option available with—books having 64 pages or fewer. Withstands fairly rugged use. Inexpensive.

Cerlox or Spiral Binding. Cerlox is a plastic ring binding in which each ring is separate from the other rings. It comes in a few standard colours and the spine edge of the Cerlox rings can be printed. Can be used for books of up to about 450 pages. Not durable, and not the best looking binding. Inexpensive.

When a book is wiro-bound or spiral bound, a continuous wire is woven through the spine edge of the pages to hold the book together. The wire can be coloured or clear and, like Cerlox binding, can be used with a few pages or many pages.

Often used in cookbooks because it allows the book to lie flat when in use. Durable and costly.

Perfectbinding and Otabinding. Perfectbinding glues together the spine and the cover. There is a minimum number of pages that can be bound this way that varies somewhat from printer to printer, but is usually not less than 64 pages. The maximum is about 1,200 pages, but this depends on the weight of stock used. Perfectbinding is durable and relatively inexpensive. Despite the fact that the pages can snap shut when the book is opened, and the spine can become brittle with age, causing pages to drop out, perfectbinding is used for all kinds of books and is a common method of binding.

Otabinding, the type of binding we recommend, is the trade name for a type of perfectbinding in which a thin piece of fabric attached to the glue on the spine means the spine has a greater degree of flex. This allows the book pages to lie flatter when opened.

Sewn. A sewn binding literally stitches together the sections, or forms, of the book. It produces a binding that is highly durable. The pages are easy to open, lie flat when opened and won't drop out. Sewn binding is used mostly for reference books, in which long life is important, cookbooks and some children's books. To be sewn, a book must be constructed of more than one form, or section, or else there would be nothing to stitch together. Make sure your book has at least 64 pages before specifying sewn binding. Expensive compared to other forms of binding.

Finished Book Date

Your need for your book may be predicated on a certain event: a family reunion, for instance, at which you plan to distribute the book. Otherwise, you may only have a fair idea of when you'd like it—say, in plenty of time for Christmas.

Either way, you should specify a date to the printer. Whether the printer can achieve or maintain this date will depend almost entirely on you. If you have contacted the company on December 2 for your Christmas book, you're out of luck and the printer will advise you accordingly. If, however, you have planned three months or so in advance, you will have a good chance of meeting that date.

Maintaining the schedule to keep delivery on track is your job. Don't expect the printer to make up time you have lost. But if you have promised to deliver your materials as of a certain date, and you have fulfilled your part of the bargain, then the printing company should meet its commitment accordingly.

A SAMPLE REQUEST FOR QUOTATION:

Title:	Publish Your Family History
Quantity:	350, 500 and 700 copies
Trim size:	5-1/2 x 8-1/2"
Number of pages:	192
Paper: Text:	60 lb. Hibulk, cream
Paper: Cover:	10 pt. Cornwall C1S
Printing: Text:	One colour black
Printing: Cover:	Four-colour process with gloss lamination coated one-side
Preparation: Text:	Text copy as Quark XPress files on CD, Macintosh format, including all screen and printer fonts, to printer's specifications. Printer to output CD files to film. Laser proofs to accompany text files.
Preparation: Cover:	Comprehensive colour separated cover negatives imposed to printer's specification.
Binding:	Perfectbound
Delivery:	To one address in the Greater Toronto area
Taxes:	Additional

Shipping

You must decide whether your printer will be doing the delivery of the finished books or whether you are arranging it. Frankly, unless you're in the business of moving freight, you're better to let the printer look after shipping. If you are printing a sufficient quantity of books that they will be packed in cartons, on skids, make sure your receiving end can accept skids. In other words, moving skids from a transport trailer to your garage isn't going to work.

COMPARING QUOTES

Now you're ready to ask for quotations. When they come in and you've completed your comparisons, you must pick one company with which you will work. Don't try to play companies with competing quotes off one other: you'll only embarrass yourself. Your next step is to issue a purchase order, or letter, confirming your order to your supplier.

Your purchase order or letter should repeat all the specifications in the quotation, as well as the printer's quotation number (if provided). Make sure you include the total cost of all the services you're buying from the printer. A cheque may need to accompany this order; the printer will let you know.

READING THE QUOTES

If you have received competing quotes, take the time to size up the quotations carefully. Make sure that none of the specifications have been changed from your Request for Quotation. Also review whether the total cost you're looking at is "all in." Some printers provide one all-inclusive cost, while others provide separate costs for preparation (plates, etc.) and manufacturing. Since both ways of quoting are industry standards, the onus is on you to compare carefully.

You're now ready to gather together the materials you have specified in your purchase order, whether film, disk or hard copy, to allow the printer to begin the job.

THE PURCHASE ORDER FOR THIS BOOK

This is how the purchase order to the printer looked for *Publish Your Family History*:

(Printed on company letterhead.)

To:	Hume Imaging Inc.

Bill to:	Ontario Genealogical Society
Ship to:	Ontario Genealogical Society

RE: PUBLISH YOUR FAMILY HISTORY: your quote number 00000

Trim size:	5-1/2 x 8-1/2" no bleed in text
Quantity:	x copies
Preparation:	Text copy as Quark XPress files on CD, Mac format. Laser proofs to accompany text file. Printer to output files to film.
Cover:	Comprehensive colour separated cover negatives imposed to printer's specifications
Paper: Text:	60 lb. Hibulk, cream
Cover:	10 pt. C1S
Printing: Text:	Black throughout
Cover:	Four process colours, gloss lamination coated one-side
Overs:	+/- 10% accepted
Binding:	Perfectbound
Delivery Date:	March 12, 2005
Cost:	For x copies @ $x.xx = $
	GST
	Total $

WHAT TO EXPECT WHEN YOU'RE GOING ON PRESS

You've worked with your printer to deliver materials for the text and cover to specifications. Are finished books next?

Not yet. The printer takes what you have supplied and provides you with a set of blueprints or "blues," also sometimes called dyluxes, or vandykes, so you can have one final look-over before going on press. Your signature on the blues is the go-ahead to the printer, so you want to make sure you know what you're looking at and that you are satisfied with what you see.

The blues are a paper proof created from the film. Film is then used to "burn" the printing plates. Blues are in one colour: blue. All the type and all the photos look blue. You can't use blues to check four-colour printing, yet blues will still be created by the printer for pages printed in four colours in recognition that these pages exist.

IT HAPPENS TO THE PROS

There isn't be a person in publishing who doesn't have a horror story about a mistake caught at the blues stage. One of our favourites concerns a cookbook with a 50,000 copy print run being prepared for a very demanding author, which was found in blues to be missing its title page. With the error discovered mere hours before going on press, a title page had to be created, film produced and transported in the middle of the night from the film house to the publisher, who waited on the side of a lonely highway to take the film to the waiting printer. The moral: It happens. But it doesn't need to if proper thought, time and care are taken in the preparation of the book.

Because blues are produced from the film, which is one of the final stages in the printing process, it will be expensive at this point to make corrections. Every change will mean new film, and that cost adds up fast. Plus, you will lose time in creating new film, and you can lose your place in the printing queue if the process starts to drag.

So, though it may be hard to restrain yourself, looking at blues is not the time to reread the book for grammatical errors, typos or a general change of heart. That happened in Chapter 4. Blues are, however, your opportunity to do many tasks that seem pretty obvious:

- ensure all the pages are there and that they are in the right order;
- ensure all the elements that comprise each page are there: the running head or foot, folio, all the text, captions if there are any and illustrations or photos;
- ensure that there are no scratch marks, blobs of dirt or hairs on the type or illustrations, that the type is not broken; and
- ensure that all the elements for the cover are in place.

Usually the printer will supply an approval page on which you can list those pages where something has caught your eye that needs attention. Do this; it also helps to mark directly on the blue page with a big circle around the offending item, in red ink, grease pencil or china marker, what you want the printer to check on the film.

The reality is that it is difficult to consistently look at page after page without reading the text. So, it is really important to go through the blues two or three times, each time focussing on the pages and the type without being distracted by the story.

DON'T READ THIS UPSIDE DOWN!

It helps to review blues from back to front as well as from front to back, because, if your attention wanders once or twice as you go along, you know you will have really seen the end of the book too. And it also helps to look at the blues upside down. This guarantees that you won't be reading the words but that you will be looking at the elements of each page.

If all is satisfactory, it's off to press. Off to press means patience. Printers' schedules have been known to move printing to an earlier time slot, but far more frequently they move back. If you have been given a finished book date, and you should have been given this in your discussions with the printer, you'll want to check on the status of the book that day. Many understanding and sympathetic printers might call you to watch your book on press. But even then, binding does not follow immediately. So, rein in your anxiety, because soon your book will be completed. Then, with your brand-new book in one hand you can pour the champagne with the other and proudly toast your achievement.

CHAPTER 11

DISTRIBUTION

Getting your book out there is one publishing function that can be tough for the home publisher, even though your goal may not be wide distribution. It's easy enough to visit various family members who live nearby with a carload of copies of your book. That's tougher to do if they live elsewhere.

Professional publishers often use a distribution firm that puts the book in their catalogue, arranges to ship it to bookstores and collects the revenue from the stores—but that is expensive and your family history's audience will likely be small. This chapter discusses ways of getting your book out to your family and possibly beyond.

DISTRIBUTING BOOKS TO YOUR FAMILY

Your immediate family members know about the book and can't wait to see their names in print. If you're only making fifteen copies and everyone lives on the same block, getting the book out is easy enough. But if the family is scattered across the country or even around the world, you'll have to plan a bit more than you would for a Sunday barbeque.

Mail or E-mail

It is always best to start putting mailing lists together early, before the book is finished, so you'll have a better idea of how many copies to print judging by your family's level of interest. Long-distance phone calls can be time-consuming and expensive. Instead, create a mailing list of relatives; regular mail or e-mail are both entirely appropriate, depending on what you prefer. Send a short cover letter to inform them about the project. If you are selling the book, include an order form for them to send back if they wish to buy a copy. Be sure there is space for all the necessary information (name and address, number of copies). As an extra incentive, consider offering a discount price if they request a copy before a certain date. Any money you collect can go towards your printing and mailing costs.

A Book Launch

Act like the celebrated author you are and throw a party to toast your accomplishment, inviting all the family members within a reasonable travelling distance. They will probably get a kick out of such an event, and it's a fun way to distribute or sell copies—everyone will be eager to get their hands on one.

A Family Reunion

You've heard the story about the time your uncle came in second in the hotdog-eating contest. You know the tale of how cousin Percy ran into a burning building to save his pet iguana. Chances are you heard these stories at a family reunion—the traditional gathering used to catch up and to comment on how much you've grown, even if you are forty-eight years old.

Instead of planning a get-together specifically around your book, you can fit it into an upcoming reunion. The larger gatherings are planned well ahead of time, or even on a set date every year, which gives you plenty of opportunity to arrange to have your book ready for the occasion.

However, not every type of family gathering is an appropriate time to bring your book. In fact, at some events it could be considered offensive. Should you push a volume of family history at Uncle Sergio's wake? Would your sister still be pleased to have you in her wedding party if she knew you planned to set up a book-selling booth at the reception? Ask yourself these types of questions before you lug a carton of books out to your car. That's not to say that you can't mention your book—just don't make it the main focus. It's perfectly acceptable to arrange to send the book out at a later time, when you won't be taking away from someone else's important day.

REACHING A BROADER AUDIENCE

You've spent countless hours researching, writing and seeing your book through the printing and production process. Now it's time to get the book out to as many people as possible, beyond your immediate family. To reach a broader audience, here are some suggestions of avenues to explore.

Genealogical Societies

Perhaps you contacted your local genealogical society for guidance and research as you wrote. They will want to purchase your book for their collection. The Canadian Genealogy Centre at **www.genealogy.gc.ca** provides a list of genealogical societies by province. You can then search the specific society for a branch near you. These are groups of people who are passionate about genealogy and who want to bring together amateur and seasoned family history buffs. They can direct you towards those who might be interested in your book, and provide you with lists of historical societies or specific libraries with special collections.

Your Local Library or Historical Society

Especially if your family has strong roots in the community, check with your nearest library or historical society. They might be interested in purchasing a copy of your book for their collection, as a historical document and as an inspiration to fellow genealogists in the area.

Library and Archives Canada

Your family history is important and you want to be sure it has a place in the collective consciousness, not just on Aunt Rhoda's bookshelf. Library and Archives Canada (LAC), a section of the government, collects Canadian published works to preserve and document the national written heritage. Publishers, even small ones, are required to provide copies of their works to LAC. How many to provide depends on the number in print. If you've printed 101 copies or more, LAC requires that you deposit two copies in their collection; if you've printed between four and 100 copies, send them only one. You won't be paid for the books, but you will have the assurance that your work will be preserved for future generations. Visit **www.collectionscanada.ca** for their contact information and to download the proper forms.

Local Shops

If you live in a smaller town or village, or in an area that is particularly touristy, the gift shop at the local historical site might take a couple of copies of your book. A professional-looking, locally produced book would make a fine souvenir, especially if your family history is somehow tied into that site.

Your Family's Country of Origin

Your ancestors, all the way up to current family members, probably haven't all lived and died in exactly the same town. If your grandfather was a gaucho on the open plains of Argentina, or your great aunt owned a tea shop in Japan, investigate historical or genealogical societies in those countries. They might be very interested in a work that documents a family's journey from their country to another.

Genealogical Web Fora

Internet discussion boards are a popular way for those with similar interests to communicate. You can chat with fellow genealogists from around the world, share your home-publishing experiences, and maybe exchange books. You might discover other families with histories intertwined with yours, or whose stories follow similar paths. To find a relevant forum, try **www.genforum.genealogy.com** to search by country and general topic.

Your Website

You've already decided that a book is a better vehicle for your family history than a website. But if you have your own personal website, why not use it to promote your book? You could post a short excerpt to pique people's interest, and perhaps a photograph or two.

AT THE END OF THE PROCESS

Your book has been printed and distributed. You have been showered with praise and thank-you notes. The project is finished, right?

For some of you, indeed it is. But the fact that you have published your book doesn't mean that you've lost your interest in researching your family history.

Your book has likely done two things for you:

- It has put you in touch with obscure family members, who may well have information on the family that was not previously available to you.
- It has aroused the interest of the other members of your family who are interested in family history, and they have sent you corrections and missing scraps of information.

Once the book is over and done with, it is time to get back to your hobby, organizing the new information as it comes in, filling in gaps and extending your knowledge of other branches of the family.

You might want to start tracking that new information on a website so that others in the family who are interested can help you with your research.

Or, more likely, you can start quietly planning what will go into Volume 2.

And even Volume 3.

Sample 8 1/2 x 11" book size professional grid, binding on 11" edge.

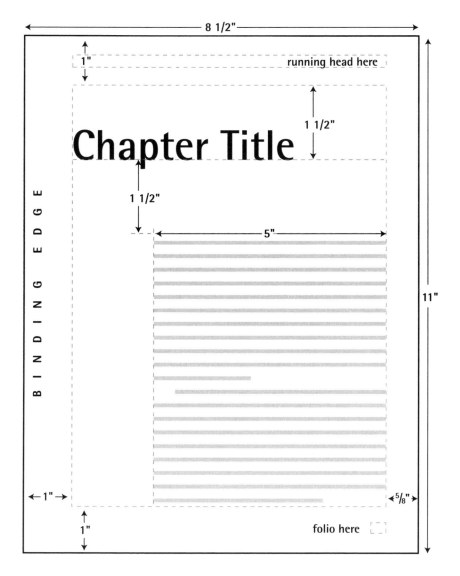

Sample 8 1/2 x 11" book size simple grid,
binding on 11" edge.

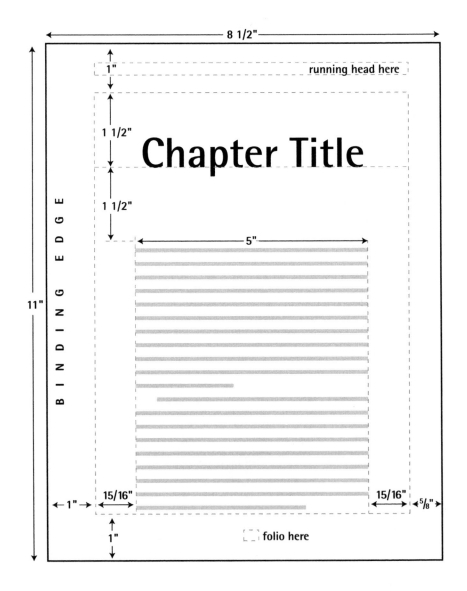

Sample 8 1/2 x 11" book size professional grid, binding on 8 1/2" edge.

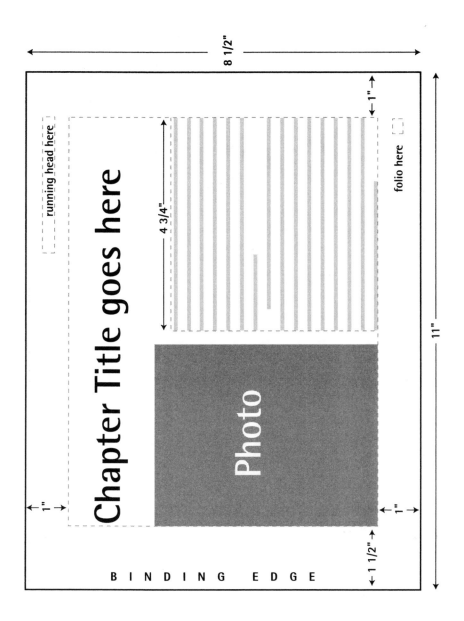

Sample 6 x 9" book size professional grid, binding on 9" edge.

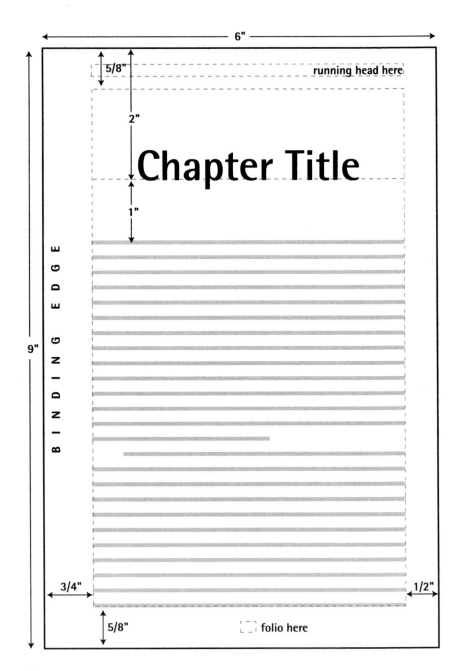

6 x 9" grid continued.

6 x 9" grid continued.

Sample 8 x 8" book size professional grid.

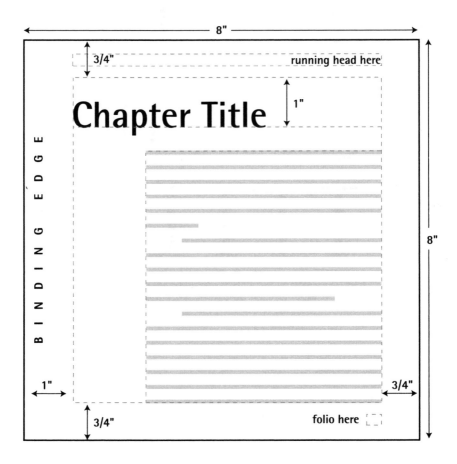

YOUR BOOK TITLE

YOUR NAME

Typeface: Trajan

YOUR BOOK
TITLE

YOUR NAME

Typeface: Trajan

INDEX